Natural Opium

Natural Opium

SOME TRAVELERS' TALES

Diane Johnson

ALFRED A. KNOPF   NEW YORK   1993

THIS IS A BORZOI BOOK
PUBLISHED BY ALFRED A. KNOPF, INC.

Copyright © 1992 by Diane Johnson
All rights reserved under International and Pan-American
Copyright Conventions. Published in the United States
by Alfred A. Knopf, Inc., New York, and simultaneously
in Canada by Random House of Canada Limited, Toronto.
Distributed by Random House, Inc., New York.

Portions of this work were originally published in
The New Yorker, Threepenny Review, and *Vanity Fair.*

ISBN 0-679-41346-4
LC 92-54287

Manufactured in the United States of America
First Edition

For J., the amiable traveler

Another important difference between tourist and traveller is that the former accepts his own civilization without question; not so the traveller, who compares it with the others, and rejects those elements he finds not to his liking.
                    PAUL BOWLES, *The Sheltering Sky*

CONTENTS

ACKNOWLEDGMENTS

My heartfelt thanks to the many hospitable friends in foreign lands, to the American Academy of Arts and Letters for the Harold and Mildred Strauss Living Award that has given me the freedom to travel and much else, and to the Bellagio Study Center of the Rockefeller Foundation for the refuge where some of these stories were written.

Paul Bowles, in *The Sheltering Sky*, described the difference between a tourist and a traveler:

> The difference is partly one of time, he would explain. Whereas the tourist generally hurries back home at the end of a few weeks or months, the traveller, belonging no more to one place than to the next, moves slowly, over periods of years, from one part of the earth to another.

There are books for tourists, but it has always seemed to me that few have been written about the existential condition of *being a traveler*. Anyone who has traveled has said, in the middle of some desert or in a moment of intense alienation in a souk, "Why am I here?" We know that travel is broadening or restorative, or that some inner compulsion we cannot explain prompts us to do it, or that it has to do with escaping from our quotidian lives. But how? Why do we do it? What are the lessons of travel? I have tried to account for those moments of travel ennui or traveler's panic we all have felt: the sheer inability to eat another wonton, the desperate wish to be transported by instantaneous space/time travel into one's own bed. Travel brings us as nothing else does to a sense of ourselves. When are we more ourselves than when traveling, feeling the deep shame of that instant when we hear the plain accents of a compatriot over the differently cadenced voices in a foreign airport, or confronting in ourselves some trace of our national puritanism, of our fatal tendency to rattle on to strangers, of our American need to be liked? There is also the strange dynamic between the traveler and the locals; we are moved by them if their condition is pitiable or primitive, and find them rude and strange if their lives are more orderly and sumptuous than ours, in European capitals or on the racecourses of Argentina. In either case the actual existence of these people is irrelevant to the passions of pity or envy they arouse in us, as we are irrelevant to them. The action of travel is all on the traveler—unless we happen to be carrying measles to the Amazon, or hard currency.

As a child my favorite books were *Around the World with Bob and Betty* (which I have looked for in vain for my own children) and Richard Henry Dana's *Two Years Before the Mast*. I was a landlocked child of the prairie, and it was not the sea that drew me (though it had as an idea such an appeal to my Iowa grandmother that she determined not to die until she had seen it: she traveled to California with her youngest child when she was ninety, saw it, and lived on the memory for quite a few more years). I wanted to cross the seas to view the orchards and castles on the other side, though I found that I rather hated the process of getting there—the airplane especially.

As a grown-up I have had the good luck to travel a lot, not usually as a tourist and not necessarily in places of my own choosing and almost always reluctantly, at moments when I felt that the time would be better spent at home. Some of my most interesting voyages have been as the companion of someone with an interest in medicine in the third world, someone invited to distant places to advise or study. While this has not justified my presence there, it has left me free to wander in foreign bazaars unattended by tour leaders and guides. Some of these travels have in fact coincided with the usual tourist trail: Bangkok or Cairo, places "cram-full of littering Venezuelans, peevish Swiss, Norwegian back-packers yodelling in restaurant booths, Saudi businessmen getting their dresses caught in revolving doors and Bengali remittance men in their 25th year of graduate school pestering fat blonde Belgian au pair girls," as P. J. O'Rourke found them. But there is instruction in viewing other travelers, too.

My own unfocused wanderings (for no one has ever asked me for my impressions) have left me with some views about the oddness of travel, especially the oddness of its effect on the traveler. For we know we have been changed by our trips, though we seldom can say how. And our friends certainly do not see it—if indeed, as Martha Gelhorn noticed, we can make them listen to our tales: "People will talk about the weather rather than hear our glowing reports on Copenhagen, the Grand Canyon, Katmandu." She adds, as we have noted, that only the disasters seem to interest. Or your friends seize the chance to tell you their travel tales in return, for they too have been changed by their week in Morocco, their summer in Plan-de-la-Tour.

The tales that follow, then, chronicle some aspects of being a traveler in far-flung places, places I hope in themselves will interest the reader. The French are now speaking of "auto-fiction," by which the teller of true stories avails herself of some of the rights of the novelist to tidy and pace the account. I have changed many of the names of people (in some cases for their protection); but the names of the hotels are true.

The list of useful travel items come from Ruth Anseh. The horrible congressmen were really from Florida, but were overheard as they lounged around at the Kahala Hilton in Honolulu. And I have taken some small liberties with chronology, sometimes telescoping the events of more than one visit into one account.

Great Barrier Reef

Marco Polo could explain or imagine explaining that what he sought was always something lying ahead, and even if it was a matter of the past it was a past that changed gradually as he advanced on his journey.

ITALO CALVINO, *Invisible Cities*

The motel had smelled of cinder block and cement floor, and was full of Australian senior citizens off a motor coach, but when we waked up in the morning a little less jet-lagged, and from the balcony could see the bed of a tidal river, with ibises and herons poking along the shallows, and giant ravens and parrots in the trees—trees strangling with monstera vines, all luridly beautiful—then we felt it would be all right.

But then when we went along to the quay, I felt it wouldn't. The ship, the *Dolphin*, was smaller than one could have imagined. Where could sixteen people possibly sleep? Brown stains from rusted drain spouts spoiled the hull. Gray deck paint splattered the ropes and ladders, orange primer showed through the chips. Wooden crates of lettuce and cabbages were stacked on the deck, and a case of peas in giant tin cans. This cruise had been J.'s idea, so I tried not to seem reproachful or shocked at the tiny, shabby vessel. But I am not fond of travel in the best of circumstances—inconvenient displacements punctuated by painful longings to be home. For J., travel is natural opium.

J. was on his way to a meeting in Singapore of the International Infectious Disease Council, a body of eminent medical specialists from different lands who are charged with making decisions about diseases: Should the last remaining smallpox virus be destroyed? What was the significance of a pocket of polio in Sri Lanka? Could leprosy be finished off with a full-bore campaign in the spring? Was tuberculosis on the way back now via AIDS victims? What about measles in the third world? I had not realized until I took up with J. that these remote afflictions were still around, let alone that they killed people in the millions. A professor of medicine, J. did research on the things that infected their lungs.

He had always longed to visit the Great Barrier Reef. Afterward he would give some lectures in Sydney and Wellington, and we planned en route to indulge another whim: skiing in New Zealand in the middle of summer, just to say we'd skied in August and to bribe me to come along, for I will go anywhere to ski, it is the one thing. For me, too, the voyage was one of escape from California after some difficult times, and was to be—what was unspoken by either of us—a sort of trial honeymoon (though we were not married) on which we would discover whether we were suited to live together by subjecting ourselves to that most serious of tests: traveling together.

A crewman named Murray, a short, hardy man with a narrow Scots face and thick Aussie accent, showed us our stateroom. It had been called a stateroom in the brochure. Unimaginably small, two foam mattresses on pallets suspended from the wall, and a smell. Tall J. couldn't stand all the way up in it. The porthole was seamed with salt and rust. Across the passage, the door of another stateroom was open, but that one was a large, pretty room, with mahogany and nautical brass fittings, and a desk, and the portholes shone. It was the one, certainly, that had been pictured in the brochure.

"This one here, the Royal, was fitted for Prince Charles, Prince of Wales, when he come on this voyage in nineteen seventy-four," Murray said.

"How do you book the Royal?" I asked.

"First come, first serve," Murray told us. Australian, egal-itarian, opposed to privilege.

Up on deck, thinking of spending five days on the *Dolphin*, I began to be seized by emotions of panic and pain I couldn't explain. They racketed about in my chest, my heart beat fast, I felt as if a balloon was blowing up inside me, squeezing up tears and pressing them out of my eyes, and thrusting painful words up into my throat, where they lodged. What was the matter with me? Usually I am a calm person (I think); five days is not a lifetime; the aesthetics of a mattress, or its comfort either, is not a matter for serious protests. A smell of rotten water sloshing somewhere inside the hull could be gotten used to. Anyone could eat tinned peas five days and survive, plenty of people in the world were glad to get tinned peas; I knew all that. I knew I wasn't reacting appropriately, and was sorry for this querulous fit of passion. Maybe it was only jet lag.

All the same, I said to J., "I just can't," and stared trag-ically at the moorings. He knew, of course, that I could and probably would, but he maintained an attitude of calm sympathy.

"You've been through a rough time," he said. "It's the court thing you're really upset about." Maybe so. The court thing, a draining and frightening lawsuit, had only been a week ago, and now here we were a hemisphere away.

The other passengers came on board, one by one or two by two. Cases clattered on the metal gangs. To me only one person looked possible—a tall, handsome, youngish man with scholarly spectacles and a weathered yachting cap. The rest were aged and fat, plain, wore shapeless brown or navy blue coat-sweaters buttoned over paunches, had gray perms and bald spots, and they all spoke in this accent I disliked, as if their vowels had been slammed in doors. They spoke like cats, I thought: *eeeooooow*. Fat Australians, not looking fond of nature, why were they all here?

"Why are these people here?" I complained to J. "What do they care about the Great Barrier Reef?"

"It's a wonder of the world, anyone would want to see it," J. said, assuming the same dreamy expression he always wore when talking about or thinking about the Great Barrier Reef, so long the object of his heart.

I hated all the other passengers. On a second inspection, besides the youngish man, only a youngish couple, Dave and Rita, looked promising, but then I was infuriated to learn that Dave and Rita were Americans—we hadn't come all this way to be cooped up for five days in a prison of an old Coast Guard cutter with other Americans, and, what was worse, Rita and Dave had drawn the Prince Charles cabin, and occupied it as if by natural right, Americans expecting and getting luxury.

Of course I kept these overwrought feelings to myself. No Australian complained. None appeared unhappy with the ship, no satirical remark, no questioning comment marred their apparent delight with the whole ship-shape of things, the cabins, even the appalling lunch, which was under way as soon as the little craft was under way, pointing itself east toward the open sea out of McKay Harbor.

After we lost sight of land, this mood of desperate resentment did not disappear, as J. had predicted, but deepened. It was more than the irritability of a shallow, difficult person demanding comfort, it was a failure of spirit, inexplicable and unwarranted on this bright afternoon. How did these obese Australian women, these stiff old men, clamber so uncomplainingly below deck to their tiny cells, careen along the railings laughing crazily as they tripped on ropes?

Doubtless one would fall and the voyage would be turned back. When I thought of the ugliness of the things I had just escaped from—the unpleasant divorce, the custody battle, the hounding of lawyers and strangers—only to find myself here, really unmanageable emotions made me turn my face away from the others.

Dinner was tinned peas, and minted lamb overdone to a gray rag, and potatoes. J. bought a bottle of wine from the little bar, which the deckhand Murray nimbly leapt behind, transforming himself into waiter or bartender as required. We sat with the promising young man, Mark, and offered him some wine, but he said he didn't drink wine. He was no use, he was very, very prim, a bachelor civil servant from Canberra, with a slight stammer, only handsome and young by some accident, and would someday be old without changing, would still be taking lonely cruises, eating minted lamb, would still be unmarried and reticent. He had no conversation, had never been anywhere, did not even know what we wanted from him. Imagining his life, I thought about how sad it was to be him, hoping for whatever he hoped for, but not hoping for the right things, content to eat these awful peas, doomed by being Australian, and even while I pitied him I found him hopeless. Even J., who could talk to anyone, gave up trying to talk to him, and, feeling embarrassed to talk only to each other as if he weren't there, we fell silent and stared out the windows at the rising moon along the black horizon of the sea.

There didn't seem a way, in the tiny cabin, for two normal-sized people to exist, let alone to make love; there was no space that could accommodate two bodies in any position. Our suitcases filled half the room. With summer clothing, our proper suits to wear in Wellington and Sydney, and bulky ski clothes of quilted down, we were ridiculously encumbered with baggage. It seemed stupid now. We were obliged to stow our bags and coats precariously on racks overhead, our duffel bags sleeping at the feet of our bunks like lumpy interloper dogs. J. took my hand comfortingly in the dark across the space between the two bunks before he dropped off to sleep; I lay awake, seized with a terrible fit of traveler's panic, suffocating with fearful visions of fire, of people in prison cells or confined in army tanks, their blazing bodies emerging screaming from the holds of ships to writhe doomed on the ground, their stick limbs ringed in flame, people burned in oil splashed on them from the holds of rusted ships, and smells of sewers, smells of underground, the slosh of engine fuel from the hell beneath.

As is so often the traveler's fate, nothing on the cruise was as promised or as we had expected. The seedy crew of six had tourist-baked smiles and warmed-over jokes. There was a little faded captain who climbed out of his tower to greet us now and then, and a sort of Irish barmaid, Maureen, who helped Murray serve the drinks. The main business of the passage seemed to be not the life of the sea nor the paradise of tropical birds on Pacific shores nor the balmy water but putting in at innumerable islands to look at souvenir shops. J., his mind on the Great Barrier Reef, which we were expected to reach on the fourth day, sweetly bore it all, the boredom and the endless stops at each little island, but I somehow couldn't conquer my petulant dislike.

It fastened, especially, on our shipmates. Reluctantly I learned their names, in order to detest them with more precision: Don and Donna from New Zealand, Priscilla from Adelaide—portly, harmless old creatures, as J. pointed out. Knowing that the derisive remarks that sprang to my lips

only revealed me as petty and querulous to good-natured J.,
I didn't speak them aloud.

But it seemed to me that these Australians only wanted
to travel to rummage in the souvenir shops, though these
were all alike from island to island: Dream Island, Hook
Island—was this a cultural or a generation gap? I brooded
on the subject of souvenirs—why they should exist, why
people should want them, by what law they were made to
be ugly—shells shaped like toilets, a row of swizzle sticks
in the shapes of women's silhouetted bodies, thin, fatter, fat,
with bellies and breasts increasingly sagging as they gradu-
ated from SWEET SIXTEEN to SIXTY. I was unsettled to
notice that the one depicting a woman of my age had a
noticeably thickened middle. These trinkets were everywhere.
I watched a man buy one, a fat one, and hand it to his wife.
"Here, Mother, this one's you," he said. Laughter a form of
hate. It was not a man from our ship, luckily, or I would
have pushed him overboard. I brooded on my own complicity
in the industry of souvenirs, for didn't I buy them myself?
The things I bought—the (I liked to think) tasteful baskets
and elegant textiles I was always carting home—were these
not just a refined form of souvenir for a more citified sort of
traveler?

Statuettes of drunken sailors, velvet pictures of island
maidens, plastic seashell lamps made in Taiwan. What contempt the people who think up souvenirs have for other
people. Yet our fellow passengers plunked down money with
no feeling of shame. They never walked on the sand or looked
at the colors of the bright patchwork birds rioting in the
palm trees. Besides us, only the other Americans, Rita and
Dave, did this. It was Dave who found the perfect helmet
shell—a regular treasure, the crew assured them, increasingly

rare—protected, even, you weren't supposed to carry them away, but who was looking? I wanted it to have been J. who got it.

Each morning, each afternoon, we stopped at another island. This one was Dream Island. "It's lovely, isn't it, dear?" Priscilla said to me. "People like to see a bit of a new place, the shopping, they have different things to make it interesting." But it wasn't different, it was the same each day: The crew hands the heavy, sacklike people grunting down into rowboats, and hauls them out onto a sandy slope of beach. Up they trudge toward a souvenir shop. This one had large shells perched on legs, and small shells pasted in designs on picture frames, and earrings made of shells, and plastic buckets, and plastic straw hats surrounded with fringe, and pictures of hula dancers.

"I don't care, I do hate them," I ranted passionately to J. "I'm right to hate them. They're what's the matter with the world, they're ugly consumers, they can't look at a shell unless it's coated in plastic, they never look at the sea—why are they here? Why don't they stay in Perth and Adelaide—you can buy shells there, and swizzle sticks in the shape of hula girls." Of course J. hadn't any answer for this, of course I was right.

I wandered onto the strand of beach and took off my shoes, planning to wade. Whenever I was left alone I found myself harking back to the court hearing, my recollections just as sharp and painful as a week ago. I couldn't keep from going over and over my ordeal, and thinking of my hated former husband, not really him so much as his lawyer, Waxman, a man in high-heeled boots and aviator glasses. I imagined him here on Dream Island. He has fallen overboard at the back of the ship. I am the only one to notice, and I have the power to cry out for rescue but I don't. Our eyes meet; he is down in the water, still wearing the glasses. I imagine his expression of surprise when he realizes that I'm not going to call for help. What for him had been a mere legal game, a job, would cost him his life. He had misjudged me. The ship speeds along. We are too far away to hear his cries.

It was the third day and we had set down at Happy Island. Here we had to wade across a sandbar. This island had goats grazing. "This is the first we've gotten wet," I bitterly complained. We stood in ankle-deep water amid queer gelatinous seaweed. I had wanted to swim, to dive, to sluice away the court and the memories but hadn't been permitted to because these waters, so innocently beautiful, so seductively warm, were riddled with poisonous creatures, deadly toxins, and sharks.

"Be careful not to pick up anything that looks like this," the first mate, Murray, warned us, showing us a harmless-looking little shell. "The deadly cone shell. And the coral, be careful a' that, it scratches like hell. One scratch can take over a year to heal. We have some ointment on board, be sure to tell one of the crew if you scratch yourself."

From here, I looked back at the ship, and, seeing the crew watching us, I suddenly saw ourselves, the passengers, with the crew's eyes—we were a collection of thick bodies, mere cargo to be freighted around, slightly volatile, likely to ferment, like damp grain, and give trouble—difficult cargo that sent you scurrying unreasonably on tasks, boozed, got itself cut on coral, made you laugh at its jokes. I could see that the crew must hate us.

Yet, a little later, I came upon Murray tying up a fishhook for old George, whose fingers were arthritic. Murray was chatting to him with a natural smile. I studied them. Perhaps

Murray by himself was a man of simple good nature, but the rest, surely, hated us. The captain, staring coolly out from his absurd quarterdeck, made no pretense of liking us, seemed always to be thinking of something else, not of this strange Pacific civilization of Quonset huts and rotting landing barges and odd South Sea denizens strangely toothless, beyond dentistry, beyond fashion, playing old records over and over on PR systems strung through the palms. You felt the forlornness of these tacky little islands that should have been beautiful and serene. I even wondered if we would ever get back to America again. Not that I wanted to. America was smeared with horrible memories, scenes of litigation. Why shouldn't J. and I simply stay here? Why—more important—was I not someone who was able, like the lovely goat that grazed on the slope near here, to gaze at the turquoise sea and enjoy the sight of little rose-colored parrots wheeling in the air? Why was I not, like a nice person, simply content to be, to enjoy beauty and inner peace? Instead I must suffer, review, quiver with fears and rages—the fault, I saw, was in myself, I was a restless, peevish, flawed person. How would I be able to struggle out of this frame of mind? Slipping on the sandy bank, I frightened the little goat.

By the third day I began to notice a sea change in our shipmates, who had begun in sensible gabardines and print dresses, but now wore violently floral shirts and dresses, and were studded with shells—wreaths of shells about their necks and at their ears, hats with crabs and gulls embroidered on. By now I knew a bit more about them. They were all travelers—George and Nettie, Fred and Polly, had been friends for forty years, and spent a part of each year, now that they were all retired, traveling in Europe in their caravans. Dave and Rita were both schoolteachers, and Rita raised Great Danes. Priscilla was going along on this cruise with her brother Albert because Albert had just lost his wife. Mark was taking his annual vacation. Don and Donna were thinking of selling their Auckland real estate business and buying a sailboat to live on and sail around the world. J. told me that George was a sensitive and sweet man who had lived his whole life in Australia and only now in his retirement had begun to see something of the world. "And he says that the most beautiful place in the world is someplace near Split, in Yugoslavia, and if I take you there, my darling, will you for God's sake cheer up now?" But I couldn't.

Tonight we were dining ashore, in a big shed on Frenchie's Island, in a shabby tin building. Music was already playing on loudspeakers. Groups of people from other ships or hotels strolled around carrying drinks. A smell of roasted sausages, someone singing "Waltzing Matilda" in the kitchen at the back. The *Dolphin* passengers were lined up at the bar and in the souvenir shop. In the big hangar of a room little tables encircled a dance floor, and at one end a microphone stood against a photo mural of the South Seas, as if the real scene outdoors were not evocative. The sun lowered across the pink water, setting in the east, and the water in the gentle lagoon was as warm as our blood. "I wish a hurricane would come and blow it all away," I said to J.

When the diners had tipped their paper plates into a bin, they began to sing old American songs. Sitting outside, I could hear Maureen singing "And Let Her Sleep Under the Bar." Then came canned music from a phonograph, and people began to dance—the ones who were not too decrepit. I tried to hear only the chatter of the monkeys or parrots in the palm trees, innocent creatures disturbed by the raucous humans. J. was strangely cheerful and shot some pool with a New Zealander, causing me all of a sudden to think, with a chill of disapproval, that J., possibly, was an Australian at heart and that I ought not to marry him or I would end up in a caravan in Split. His good looks and professional standing were only a mask that concealed . . . simplicity.

It didn't surprise me that people liked the handsome and amiable J.; it didn't even surprise me that they seemed to like me. I had concealed my tumult of feelings, and I was used to being treated by other people with protective affection, if only because I am small. This in part explained why the courtroom, and its formal process of accusation, its focus on myself as a stipulated bad person, had been such a shock. It was as if a furious mob had come to smash with sticks my porcelain figure of my self. I had a brief intimation that the Australians with their simple friendliness could put me back together if I would let them, but I would rather lie in pieces for a while.

The moon was full and golden. "What a beautiful, beautiful night," said Nettie from Adelaide, the sister of George, coming out onto the beach. Who could disagree? Not even I. The ship on the moonlit water lapped at anchor, resting, awaiting them, looking luxurious and serene. J. came out and showed us the Southern Cross. At first I couldn't see it, all constellations look alike to me, I have never been able to see the bears or belts or any of it. But now, when J. turned my chin, I did see it, and it did look like a cross.

In the night I had another dream, in which the lawyer had said, "Isn't it true that you have often left your children while you travel?" He had been looking not at me but at a laughing audience. He was speaking over a microphone. The audience wore plastic, fringed hats.

"Not willingly, no," I had said. "Not often."

"How many times did you go on trips last year and leave them at home?"

"Oh, six, I don't know."

"That's not often?"

"Just a day or two each time. A man takes a business trip, you don't call it leaving, or 'often.' " But I was not allowed to speak or explain.

"We're looking at how often you are in fact away from your children."

Here I had awakened, realizing that it was all true, it wasn't just a dream, it was what had happened, not of course the audience in plastic hats. Even though in the end I had been vindicated, I still felt sticky with the encumbrance of their father's hate. All I had wanted was to be free and now I was so soiled with words spoken at me, about me, by strangers, by lawyers I had never seen before, who had never seen me. It didn't seem fair that you could not prevent being the object of other people's emotions, you were not safe anywhere from their hate—or from their love, for that matter. You were never safe from being invaded by their feelings when you wanted only to be rid of them, free, off, away.

In the morning I had wanted to swim, to wash in the sea, to wash all this stuff off, splash; my longing must have been clear, because Cawley, the other deckhand, laughed at me. "Not here you don't, love," he said. "There's sharks here as long as a boat."

The captain, Captain Clarke, made one of his few visits. He had kept aloof in the little pilot cabin above, though he must have slipped down to the galley to eat, or maybe the crew took him his food up there. Now he invited his passengers two by two to his bridge. When people were tapped, they hauled themselves up the metal ladder, helped by Cawley or Murray, then would come down looking gratified. Alfred, who went up alone, suggested that he had helped avoid a navigational accident.

J. and I were invited on the morning of the fourth day, the day we were to arrive at the reef itself in the late afternoon. I went up despite myself. Captain Clarke was a thin, red-haired man sitting amid pipes and charts. He let us take the wheel, and showed us the red line that marked our route through the labyrinth of islands shown on a chart. His manner was grave, polite, resigned. No doubt these visits were dictated by the cruise company.

"But there are thousands of islands between here and the Great Barrier Reef!" said J., studying the charts.

"Souvenir shops on every one," I couldn't help saying. J. fastened me with a steady look in which I read terminal exasperation.

"These islands are not all charted," said the captain. "The ones that are were almost all charted by Captain Cook himself, after he ran aground on one in seventeen seventy. He was a remarkable navigator. He even gave names to them all. But new ones are always being found. I've always hoped to find one myself."

"What would you name it?" J. asked.

"I would give it my name, or, actually, since there is already a Clarke Island, I would name it for my wife, Laura, Laura Clarke Island, or else for Alison, my daughter."

"Do you keep your eyes open for one?"

"I mean to get one," he said.

When we went down to the deck again, Maureen was gazing at the waves. "It's getting choppy," she observed, unnecessarily, for the boat had begun to rear up like a prancing horse.

"Right, we probably won't make it," Murray agreed.

"What do you mean?" I asked, alarmed by the tinge of satisfaction that underlay their sorry looks.

"To the reef. No point in going if the sea's up, like it's coming up, washed right up, no use going out there. If it's like this, we put in at Hook Island instead."

Astonished, I looked around to see if J., or anyone else, was listening. No, or not worried, would just as soon have Hook Island. They continued to knit and read along the deck, which now began to heave more forcefully, as if responding to the desire of the crew to return to port without seeing the great sight.

"How often does it happen that you don't go to the reef?" I asked, heart thundering. The point of all this, and J.'s dream, was to go to the reef, and now they were casually dismissing the possibility.

"Oh, it happens more often than not. This time of year, you know. Chancy, the nautical business is."

"Come out all this way and not see it?" I insisted, voice rising.

"Well, you can't see it if the waves are covering it up, can you? You can bump your craft into it, but you can't see it. Can you?"

"I don't know," cried I. "I don't even know what it is." But the shape of things was awfully clear; given the slightest excuse, the merest breeze or ripple, the *Dolphin* would not take us to the Great Barrier Reef, and perhaps had never meant to. I thought in panic of not alerting J., but then I rushed to tell him. He put down his book, his expression aghast, and studied the waves.

The midday sky began to take on a blush of deeper blue, and, now that our attention was called to it, the sea seemed to grow dark and rough before our eyes. Where moments before it had been smooth enough to row, we now began to pitch. The report of the prow smacking the waves made me think of cannons, of Trafalgar. In defiance of the rocking motion, the Australian passengers began to move around the cabin and along the deck, gripping the railings, looking trustfully at the sky and smiling. Their dentures were white as teacups.

"Christ," said Murray, "one of these bloody old fools will break a hip. Folks, why don't you sit down?" Obediently, like children, the Australians went inside the main cabin and sat in facing rows of chairs. Despite the abrupt change in the weather, the ship continued its course out to sea. J. and I anchored ourselves in the prow, leaning against the tool chest, resolutely watching the horizon, not the bounding deck beneath our feet, a recommended way to avoid seasickness. In twenty minutes the sea had changed altogether, from calm to a thing that threw the little ship in the air. We felt as if we were slithering along the back of a sea monster who toiled beneath us.

The dread specter of seasickness was promptly among us. The captain, rusty haired, pale eyed, as if his eyes had bleached with sea wind, climbed off the bridge and glanced inside the cabin at his passengers.

"Oh, please, they want to go, they'll be all right," I called to him, but the words were swept off by the wind.

The others were so occupied with the likelihood of nausea that they hadn't grasped that the ship might turn back, and they seemed rather to be enjoying the drama of getting seasick. Every few minutes someone would get up, totter out to the rail, retch over it, and return to the laughter and commiseration of the others. The friendly thing was to be sick, so I was contrarily determined not to be, and J. was strong by nature. One of the Australians, Albert, gave us a matey grin as he lurched over our feet toward a bucket. I looked disgustedly away, but J. wondered aloud if he should be helping these old folks.

"Of course they'll use this as an excuse for not going," I was saying bitterly. These barfing Australian senior citizens would keep us from getting to the Great Barrier Reef. My unruly emotions, which had been milder today, now plumped around in my bosom like the smacking of the boat on the waves. J. watched the Australians screaming with laughter, and telling each other, "That's right, barf in the bin."

"This is a rough one," Albert said, and pitched sharply against the cabin, so that J. leapt up to catch him. Murray, tightening ropes, called for him to go back in the cabin.

"Tossed a cookie meself." He grinned at J. and me.

"We don't think it's so rough," I said.

"I've seen plenty rougher," Murray agreed. "Bloody hangover is my problem."

When the captain leaned out to look down at the deck below him, I cried, "Oh, we just have to go to the reef, we have to! Oh, please!"

"What's the likelihood this sea will die down?" J. shouted to the captain. The captain shrugged. I felt angry for the first time at J., as if he were a magnet. It was unfair, I knew, to say it was J.'s fault—the storm, the tossing sea, the *Dolphin*, and of course the rest. J. who had signed us up for this terrible voyage, during which we would be lost at sea, before reaching the Great Barrier Reef, whatever it was, and who had caused the sea to come up like this.

All J.'s fault. If I ever saw the children again, it would be a miracle, or else them saying in after years, Our mother perished on the high seas somewhere off Australia. What would they remember of me? The sight of the boiling waves, now spilling over the bow, now below us, made me think of throwing myself in—just an unbidden impulse trailing into my mind, the way I half-thought, always, of throwing my keys or my sunglasses off bridges. Of course I wouldn't do it.

The ship pitched, thrust, dove through the waters. Yet we had not turned back. "Whoooeee," the Aussies were screaming inside the lounge. Life was like this, getting tossed around, and then, right before the real goal is reached, something, someone, makes you turn back.

"J., don't let them turn back," I said again, for the tenth time, putting all the imperative passion I knew into my voice. Without hearing me, J. was already climbing the ladder to the bridge. I looked at my fingers whitely gripping the rope handle on the end of the tool chest. A locker slid across the deck, back, across, back, and once, upon the impact of a giant wave, a dead fish stowed in it sloshed out onto the deck. Then, in the wind, I heard Murray's thin voice call out, "It's all right, love, we're going to the reef! The captain says we're going to the reef!"

As abruptly as the storm had started, it subsided meekly, the sky once more changed color, now to metallic gray, lighter at the horizon, as if it were dawn. Ahead of us an indistinguishable shape lay in the water like the back of a submerged crocodile, a vast bulk under the surface. The captain had stopped the engines, and we drifted in the water. "The reef, the reef!" cried the Australians, coming out on deck. I shouted too. The crew began to busy themselves with readying the small boats, and the other passengers came boisterously out of the cabin, as if nothing had been wrong. "Ow," they said, "that was a bit of a toss."

"You'll have two hours on the reef, not more," the captain

told us before we climbed again into the rowboats. "Because of the tide. If you get left there at high tide, if we can't find you, well, we don't come back. Because you wouldn't be there." The Australians laughed at this merry joke.

J. handed me out of the boat and onto the reef. My first step on it shocked me. For I had had the idea of coral, hard and red, a great lump of coral sticking out of the ocean, a jagged thing that would scratch you if you fell on it, that you could chisel into formations dictated by your own mind. We had heard it was endangered, and I had imagined its destruction by divers with chisels, carrying off lumps at a time.

Instead it was like a sponge. It sank underfoot, it sighed and sucked. Shocked, looking down, I could see that it was entirely alive, made of eyeless formations of cabbagey creatures sucking and opening and closing, yearning toward tiny ponds of water lying on the pitted surface, pink, green, gray, viscous, silent. I moved, I put my foot here, then hurriedly there, stumbled, and gashed my palm against something rough.

"Where should you step? I don't want to step on the things," I gasped.

"You have to. Just step as lightly as you can," J. said.

"It's alive, it's all alive!"

"Of course. It's coral, it's alive, of course," J. said. He had told me there were 350 species of coral here, along with the calcareous remains of tiny polyzoan and hydrozoan creatures that helped to form a home for others.

"Go on, J., leave me," I said, seeing that he wanted to be alone to have his own thoughts about all this marine life, whatever it meant to him. It meant something. His expression was of rapture. He smiled at me and wandered off.

I had my Minox, but I found the things beneath my feet too fascinating to photograph. Through the viewer of my camera they seemed pale and far away. At my feet in astonishing abundance they continued their strange life. I hated to tread on them, so at length stood like a stork, and aimed the camera at the other passengers.

These were proceeding cautiously, according to their fashion, over the strange surface—Mark in his yachting cap, with his camera, alone; the Kiwis in red tropical shirts more brilliant than the most bright-hued creatures; even the crew, with insouciant expressions, protectively there to save their passengers from falls or from strange sea poisons that darted into the inky ponds from the wounded life beneath the feet. For the first time, I felt, seeing each behaving characteristically, that I knew them all, and even that I liked them, or at least that I liked it that I understood what they would wear and do. Travelers like myself.

I watched J. kneeling in the water to peer into the centers of the mysterious forms. Almost as wonderful as this various life was J.'s delight. He was as dazzled as if we had walked on stars, and indeed the sun shining on the tentacles, wet petals, filling the spongy holes, made things sparkle like a strange underfoot galaxy. He appeared as a long, sandy-haired, handsome stranger, separate, unknowable. I, losing myself once more in the patterns and colors, thought of nothing, was myself as formless and uncaring as the coral, all my unruly, bad-natured passions leaching harmlessly into the sea, leaving a warm sensation of blankness and ease. I thought of the Hindu doctrine of *ahimsa*, of not harming living things, and I was not harming them, I saw—neither by stepping on them nor by leaving my anger and fears and the encumbrances of real life with them. Almost as wonderful as J.'s happiness was this sense of being healed of a poisoned spirit.

At sunset we headed landward into the sun, a strange direction to a Californian, for whom all sunsets are out at sea. We would arrive at McKay at midnight—it also seemed strange that a voyage that had taken four days out would take only six hours back, something to do with the curve of the continental shelf. A spirit of triumph imbued our little party— we had lived through storms and reached a destination. People sat in the lounge labeling their rolls of film.

Maureen came along and reminded us that, as this was our last night on board, there would be a fancy dress party. When we had read this in the brochure, I had laughed. It had seemed absurd that such a little ship would give itself great liner airs. J. and I had not brought costumes. In our cabin, I asked him what he meant to wear. Since my attitude had been so resolutely one of noncompliance, he seemed surprised that I was going to participate in the dressing up. Now it seemed too churlish to object. "I know it's stupid, but how can we not?" I said. "It would be so pointed, with only sixteen of us aboard."

J. wore his ski pants, which were blue and tight, with a towel cape, and called himself Batman. I wore his ski parka, a huge, orange, down-filled garment. The others were elaborately got up, must have brought their masks and spangles with them. Rita wore a black leotard and had painted cat whiskers on her face, and Dave had a Neptune beard. Nettie wore a golden crown, and Don a harlequin suit, half purple, half green. I drew to one side and sat on the table with my feet drawn up inside J.'s parka, chin on my knees, watching the capers which now began. "I? I am a pumpkin," I explained, when they noticed the green ribbon in my hair, my stem. It wasn't much of a costume, but it was all I could think of, and they laughed forgivingly and said that it looked cute.

J. won a prize, a bottle of beer, for the best paper cutout of a cow. I was surprised, watching him with the scissors making meticulous little snips, to see how a cow shape emerged under his hands, with a beautiful delicate udder and teats, and knobs of horn. I had not thought that J. would notice a cow.

"I have an announcement," Mark said, in a strangely loud and shaky voice, one hand held up, his other hand nervously twisting his knotted cravat. The theme of his costume was not obvious.

"Excuse me, an announcement." The others smiled and shushed. "I've had word from my friend—a few months ago I had the honor to assist a friend with his astronomical observations, and I've just had word that he—we—that the comet we discovered has been accepted by the international commission. It will bear his name, and, as I had the honor to assist, I'll be mentioned too. Only a little comet, of course, barely a flash in the sky. There are millions of them, of course. There are millions of them. But . . ."

A cheer, toasts, Mark bought drinks for everybody. The crew bought drinks for the guests, dishing up from behind the little bar with the slick expertise of landside bartenders. They seemed respectful at Mark's news. I raised my glass with the rest and felt ashamed at the way I had despised Mark's life—indeed a nice life, spent exploring the heavens with a friend—how had I thought him friendless, this nice-looking young man?

"Split, Yugoslavia, is the most beautiful place on earth,"

George was telling me. "Like a travel poster. I've been almost everywhere by now, except China, but there, at Split, my heart stopped." My attention was reclaimed from my own repentant thoughts; for a second I had been thinking that he was describing a medical calamity, and I had been about to say, "How terrible!"

But no, he was describing a moment, an experience, the experience of beauty. He had the long, bald head of a statesman, but he was a farmer, now retired, from Perth. I was ashamed that it had taken me so long to see that the difference between Americans and Australians was that Americans were tired and bored, while for Australians, stuck off at the edge of the world, all was new, and they had the energy and spirit to go off looking for abstractions like beauty, and comets.

"Let me get you another one of those," George said, taking my wineglass, for a pumpkin cannot move.

"How long have you been married?" asked Nettie, smiling at me. I considered, not knowing whether I wanted to shock them by admitting that we were not married at all. "Two years," I said.

"Really?" Nettie laughed. "We all thought you was new-lyweds." Her smile was sly.

I felt myself flush inside the hot parka. The others had thought all my withdrawn unfriendliness was newlywed shy-ness and the preoccupations of love. They were giving me another chance.

"It seems like it." I laughed. I would never marry J., I thought. He was too good-natured to be saddled with a cross person like me. And yet now I wasn't cross, was at ease and warm with affection for the whole company. Don and Donna were buying champagne all around, and the crew, now that they were about to be rid of this lot of passengers, seemed sentimental and sorry, as if we had been the nicest, most amusing passengers ever.

The prize for the best costume was to be awarded by vote. People wrote on bits of paper and passed them to Maureen, who sat on the bar and sorted them. There was even a little mood of tension, people wanting to win.

"And the prize for the best costume," she paused portentously, "goes to the pumpkin!" My shipmates beamed and applauded. In the hot parka I felt myself grow even warmer with shame and affection. People of goodwill and good sense, and I had allowed a snobbish mood of accidie to blind me to it. Their white untroubled smiles.

In a wrapped paper parcel was a key ring with a plastic-covered picture of the *Dolphin*, and the words GREAT BAR-RIER REEF around the edge of it. I was seized by a love for it, would always carry it, I decided, if only as a reminder of various moral lessons I thought myself to have learned, and as a reminder of certain bad things about my own character.

"Thank you very much," I said. "I'll always keep it. And I'll always remember the *Dolphin* and all of you"—for at the moment I thought, of course, that I would. J. was looking at me with a considering air, as if to inspect my sincerity. But I was sincere.

"I know I've been a pig," I apologized to him later, as we gathered our things in the stateroom. "These people are really very sweet."

"I wonder if you'd feel like that if you hadn't gotten the prize," he said, peevishly. I was surprised at his tone. Of course it wasn't the prize, only a little key chain, after all, that had cured me, but the process of the voyage, and the mysterious power of distant places to dissolve the problems the traveler has brought along. Looking at J., I could see that, for his part, he was happy but let down, as if the excitement and happiness of seeing the reef at last, and no doubt the nuisance of my complaining, had worn him out for the moment, and serious thoughts of his coming confrontations with malaria and leprosy and pain and sadness were returning, and what he needed was a good night's sleep.

Wine

The man who first transplanted the grape of Burgundy to the Cape of Good Hope . . . never dreamt of drinking the same wine at the Cape that the same grape produced upon the French mountains . . . undoubtedly he expected to drink some sort of vinous liquor; but whether good, bad, or indifferent—he knew enough of this world to know, that it did not depend upon his choice, but that which is generally called chance. . . .

LAURENCE STERNE

The rosy-faced Canadian doctor had called for wine, and the Thai waiters, betraying a certain consternation beneath the impassive perfection of their manners, had retired to the serving area beyond double doors at the rear of the dining room, presumably to search for some. "Wine is not much drunk in Thailand," Madame Prangithornbupu explained in a low voice, embarrassed that they had not thought of it, and that it could not immediately be brought. I reflected with some satisfaction that in my travels I had at least learned that much, not to ask for wine in hot Asian countries, except in China, where the Great Wall wine is good.

"With a fabulous dinner like this, it'd be a shame not to have some wine!" Professor Harmon was exuberantly continuing. Perhaps wine snobbery had just reached Canada. Insensible to the dismay of his hosts, he was holding his hand aloft in a permanent gesture of command. The slender waiters in their gold-braided jackets peered around the doors, confirming from the lifted hand that the need still existed. The headwaiter came to whisper something discreetly to Professor Prangithornbupu, who leaned over to whisper in turn to

Mr. Kagura, the vice president for the Thailand branch of
Pan-Pac Pharmaceuticals, the Japanese drug firm, which was
paying for the elaborate dinner at one of the most expensive
hotels in Bangkok—though not *the* most expensive. J. and
I were staying at the one I liked best, the Oriental, where I
would have liked to work on my novel, sitting perhaps in
the spot where Conrad sat, watching the life along the river.
But this hotel was all right, open to the balmy night, though
the decor was like that of any hotel anywhere, with scarlet
flocked wallpaper and fake French sconces. From the dining
room we could look out at the black water, where the long
taxi boats, like gondolas, still plied, despite the hour, between this shore and the klongs, the water lapping their
cargo of musty bales and mangoes. The boats on the river
provided the only means of avoiding the insupportable, the
nearly mortal traffic of Bangkok. We had wondered that the
Thai—people so slender, small, and beautiful, everything in
their bearing suggesting happy delicacy—should allow themselves to be stifled, foundered, crushed in the worst traffic
in the world, in foully polluting taxis paralyzed between goat
carts and surreys, in private cars, buses, vans, trucks. During
the ride in from the airport, the desperate J. had leapt from
the taxi to escape, pulling me after him, and we had wandered
on foot along the frantic sidewalks, among a throng of rick-
shaws, Thai schoolchildren in their demure English uniforms,
English shoppers, and pairs of American men in holiday
clothes, escaping into the temple courtyards to gaze at smug
golden Buddhas smiling at the human folly without, and be
gazed at by the saffron-draped monks.

But the crush of Bangkok, its impenetrable traffic, and
the air—smudgy, red, and neon in the night—did not concern us here. The assembled guests were mostly members of
the International Infectious Disease Council. In the beautiful,

palm-treed jungles of the Thai countryside, there were tuberculosis, malaria, AIDS, leprosy, and dozens of other diseases caused by parasites, fungi, bacteria, and viruses. But here we were protected by the decorous rituals of Asian hospitality and international plumbing.

I had mixed feelings about the incident of the wine—on the one hand, that I was irritated at Don Harmon for not seeming to care what a lot of trouble he was putting our hosts to, and, on the other hand, that I would actually like a glass of wine, had drunk only orange juice before dinner, like the other ladies, in the Asian fashion. On my left, Mrs. Kagura, wife of the Pan-Pac Pharmaceuticals man, was telling me the details of life for an expatriate Japanese family stationed in Thailand—how hard it was to find good nannies and Japanese schools, and what a great place it was to buy jewelry if you knew what you were doing. It was a discourse one might hear from American or English foreign service wives almost anywhere. I did not despise these concerns. Mrs. Kagura was a tall, pretty woman, taller than I, with hair in a glossy black chignon, wearing an expensive silk dress, her eyelids lightly rose-shadowed, her nails a careful rose-nacre. I was struck by her worldly and modern air, not at all Japanese, could not be imagined in kimono and those little clogs. But of course all that was over, in Japan and everywhere, all is Vuitton bags and Chanel.

As J.'s new wife, wanting to do my part as a helpmate on these travels of his, I had only to learn, in several languages, to ask and answer the question How many children do you have? In the minds of doctors of whatever nation, in the minds of men in general, the notion that I might do, or be, something besides a wife and mother had never occurred. And since I wasn't anything that I could easily explain to them (I felt, in the company of people who struggle against disease), I did not feel aggrieved. "I have four," I had learned to say briskly, and change the subject: "And do you have children? How many?" If I wanted to make a startling impression on some unworldly Bulgarian, gentle Catholic Swiss, Asian, African, I could include J.'s in the count and say, "Seven."

Mrs. Kagura and I had finished that particular conversation. Four, I had said. Now Mrs. Kagura turned to me and said, "I wonder if you would mind trying on this ring?" She pulled from her slender hand a large opal and pearl ring and dropped it into my hand. My attention, which had been momentarily diverted to the drama of the wine, was returned to the elegant Japanese woman. I slipped the ring on and spread my fingers. My hand looked rather aged and stringy to me.

"I wanted to see how it would look on an older hand," said Mrs. Kagura. "It is a present for my mother." I stared at her smooth and guileless face—a woman somewhat younger than I, but not, after all, young enough to be my daughter. Even granting that perhaps "older" was meant to be some sort of compliment in the Japanese mind, I felt a subtle alteration in my opinion of Mrs. Kagura, whom until now I had been liking. It was Mrs. Kagura who had drawn attention to something that separated us, age, when it had seemed that we were the same.

A bottle had been produced, was being shown to Professor Prangithornbupu and then to Mr. Kagura, who would be paying for it, and was opened. The waiter began slowly to circle the first of the two tables of eight, offering the precious substance, which apparently was intended to serve sixteen people. I looked at the other table to see whether J. would be selfless enough to refuse it. He was. Content with his beer, he waved the waiter on. I could see the label on the bottle as the waiter came nearer: Chateau Talbot 1982. Mrs. Prangithornbupu, on my left, indicated with a word in Thai that she didn't want any. I shook my head yes, I did, and the waiter poured an ounce into my glass. Mrs. Kagura accepted some too. Another Japanese, Dr. Kora, who had unaccountably been passed over, snapped his fingers at the waiter to come back and give him some. The waiter apportioned the crimson ounces with the precision of a chemist.

"First rate," Donald Harmon said, his open, prairie-bred face beaming, lifting his glass with an expansive wave of thanks. "But we'll need another bottle," he added to the waiter. Mr. Kagura, smiling, beckoned to the waiter and directed to him a look of assent, with, perhaps, a half gesture that the waiter would be expected to understand. The waiter backed silently off between the double doors.

Presumably Don Harmon had no idea what this would cost, but I thought it was inconsiderate in any case for him to do the ordering at someone else's dinner party and felt embarrassed on behalf of North Americans generally. I could imagine his thinking—a drug company, Japanese, tons of money, what the hell—but I had learned that it cost the earth to cradle these precious bottles all the way to Asia in the hold of some ship or plane. I had ordered wine once in the Philippines, similarly innocent when I'd said, "I'll just have a glass of white wine," like any normal Californian. But J. and I had been paying for that particular supper, and when, after a long delay, some wine had been found, an ordinary California white, it had cost sixty dollars.

Remembering that made me remember other times I had thoughtlessly and inappropriately ordered wine. Once was in the Yucátan, near Tikal, where J. was working on a trial of new typhoid medicines. On a weekend, we had gone to see the Mayan ruins, getting to the excavations through the jungle, partway in an ancient DC-3, then along rutted roads in a jeep to what seemed to be the end of the earth. We were staying in what had been called a resort, a collection of simple cabins with a thatched dining room in the center, all open to the night jungle noises, insects, cricket songs, and crackle of animals in the brush. Guatemala had looked, now that I came to think of it, a lot like Thailand, but whereas the Thai had placid, complacent Buddhas, the ancient Mayas, like the Aztecs, had had malevolent, terrifying, killer-faced gods demanding human blood. It cannot be true, as the archaeologists believe, that the Mayas were peaceable and kind.

We had wandered for miles in the afternoon among the overgrown paths and raddled temples, speculating on the ancient civilization and its disappearance, on the disappearance of all civilizations, and had come along late for dinner. Had fallen asleep after our explorations, and now were hungry. We were the only people in the dining room. Between pork and chicken we had chosen chicken. "Get a bottle of red," I had whispered to J., "the white will never be cold."

"A bottle of red wine, *por favor*," J. had said, "*y agua minerale.*"

"Excuse me?"

"*Uno bottaglio*, um, of *vino tinto*," said J.

"*Sí, señor*," the young waiter had said, finally understanding J.'s approximate Spanish. An Indian, perhaps a descendant of Mayas—undoubtedly so, for this was far from cities and the spoor of the Spaniard conquerors. The faces of the people here were incarnations of the round-eyed, staring stone faces on the mossy walls of the strange ziggurats we had climbed in the afternoon.

In moments an older man appeared and said that the wine would soon arrive. However, it did not. After twenty minutes, J., whose impatience is (in my opinion) nearly his only flaw, called for beer and asked if there was a problem.

"The manager has gone for the wine, señor. Perhaps you would like your dinner before?" Something evasive in his tone.

"No, no, we'll wait for the wine," J. had said, with a dark look at me. "I wish you would learn to drink beer."

"I'm sorry, I just don't like it," I said. "Go ahead and eat." But J. waited, with punctilious, reproachful forbearance.

It was an hour before the wine arrived. We heard the screech of the car pulling up, braking fast, of feet on gravel—the wine being delivered, a sense in the air of backstage drama, urgency, relief. In the dirt-floored passage that led to the kitchen, we saw a boy, small, aged fourteen or so, carrying a bottle. It was he who had been sent out into the night. He looked at us, and my eye caught his. Soon the waiter brought the bottle, with two glasses on a tray, and then the chicken, a stringy, boiled bird in sauce, which we fell on with hungry gratitude. J. poured out two glasses of wine and tasted his.

"Ha, ha, this is sweet wine, it's Mogen David or something." He laughed at my disappointment and called for some more beer. I tasted it—sweet, syrupy, grape juice. I took mineral water.

"Surely after all that you're going to drink it?" J. said, with feigned astonishment, but with a teasing note in his voice that made me feel determined to drink it, with the appearance of enjoyment, and so I had, feeling sorry I'd asked for it, and feeling a sort of shame to be the rich gringo whose imperative command sends the poor local off into the night on an hour's drive for something she doesn't even want. J.

had not felt the same remorse. "If you operate a hotel, you expect the caprices of tourists," he had said, reasonably enough.

And then, with every sip of the horrid wine, I had felt my fury rise at J. During this period we were not yet married, and we had been quarreling about whether and when we should marry. I was reluctant. I saw marriage as going through life in an open boat, taking turns at the oars, and this metaphor revealed to me my inadequacies, the failure of my strength, little puny strokes next to J.'s strong ones, me always losing the oars. Could I yoke J. in such a galley? At other times, when love overcame the mistrust I felt toward marriage in general, and I said I was ready, it would be J. who seemed vague and reluctant. "Well, great," he would say. "Whatever. I'm sure we'll both know when the moment is right," and I would sense his lack of interest, or maybe his second thoughts. Thus whenever the subject arose, the one in a marrying mood would reproach the other, and the whole basis of our project would be called into question. It was a quarrel that bored us both a little, yet we would hear ourselves plunging into its prerehearsed lines almost without being able to help ourselves: here's why you don't really love me, here's why I don't really love you.

There was one reservation I usually kept to myself. Sometimes I thought it was hard being with someone like J., who had been assured since birth of the value and rectitude of his character, because he did indeed have a good character. On most subjects, J. and I felt differently, and, where we differed, it was almost always J. who felt correctly. Charity, understanding, and judicious calm characterized him. He gave the benefit of the doubt. He didn't panic. He was philosophical about discomfort where I railed. I held all this against him, and said so now, sipping the wine, and we were launched. Our voices rose. The waiters stared, hoping themselves invisible, at the end of the passage.

The quarrel and the Guatemalan sweet wine had given me a savage headache, and I had lain stupefied well into the morning, indifferent to the mosquitoes outside the net, listening to J. singing under a lukewarm shower on the porch of the little cabin, and to the calls of birds and jungle creatures, maybe monkeys trying to wake me. It was then I had resolved never to ask for wine where it wasn't likely to be.

But wine was everywhere. On safari, deep in the Serengeti, your outfitters brought along wine, and delicate dishes were prepared for you each evening as the sun set, and you drank French wine and watched the animals creep close to the encampment. In China I had drunk wine called Great Wall. There had been wine in the Bible, and so it was not just a European obsession pandered to by underdog nations—wine had always been.

And yet another time, asking for wine had ended badly; this was the worst time, in India. We were traveling from Delhi to Agra, on the obligatory visit to the Taj Mahal. At that moment we were in a mood of sentimental harmony, and we had expected at Agra, looking at the great building emblematic of immortal love, to feel as one. The spirits of Shah Jehan and his Mumtaz would bless us, these tutelary presences had had a meaning for us. We didn't discuss this in advance as the goal of our journey, each said only that he did want to see the Taj Mahal, it would be a shame to be in India and not see it, and each supposed that the aura of the place would, if it wasn't too touristy, speak to us, embody our emotions, move us into permanent accord, and remind us of the length of eternity.

We were riding in an uncomfortable, badly sprung, hot little car rented for the day by Vidia's father—Vidia was one of J.'s postdoctoral fellows. He had let his father know that J., his guru, was coming to India, and when J. and I got to our Delhi hotel, midmorning on a Wednesday, here were two strange, dark, short Indian men in white turbans waiting for us in the lobby, sitting in dreamy, sleepy silence on a bench—were actually asleep, perhaps, for their turbaned heads leaned one against the other like the swaying stalks of pampas grass in the tall urns of the lobby. The desk clerk had whispered, "They have been waiting for you, sir, since dawn," with a note of reproach, as if it had been J.'s fault not to have got there sooner. The men jumped up and salaamed, hands pressed together against their foreheads, and firmly they explained that all had been arranged to take the great guru to Agra.

The father, Dr. Shankar, a village general practitioner, was obliged to return to his patients, but the uncle, Mr. Shankar, would accompany us. Protestations had been useless, and now we were on our way—J. and I in the backseat of the small Indian-made car, the uncle and a driver in front.

"What will the doctor be liking for lunch? What will the doctor be liking for dinner? One has heard that whiskey will be wanted?"

"Oh, no, just a little wine"—is that how wine had come up? It seemed in retrospect unlikely that it had been I who mentioned it. Yet J. has blamed me ever since for what happened. We were stuck with the anxious, hovering, sweating, solicitous Mr. Shankar, confined together in his car, hot and terrified, and J. had been unwise enough to say, when Mr. Shankar had got out to see about something: "I wish you hadn't asked for wine." Resentment burned in my middle like something swallowed, but I couldn't say anything because here was Mr. Shankar back again.

"I have asked a gentleman I know, it is the nephew of my

brother-in-law, who is in the selling-of-liquor business, to provide some Indian wine for you, and we can stop back for it when we return to Delhi."

I gritted my teeth. It hadn't been I who had asked for wine.

We were mortally frightened at the driving, at the way the driver with his horn blaring ran up on the heels of each person toiling along the road—people yoked like animals— tailgated up to each donkey cart, up to each woman building the road from mud carried on her head, each cow arrogantly meandering, each ox, each goat, each child on a bicycle, a tide of creatures flooding, stumbling, wandering along the dusty, rutted road, the automobile darting among them like something berserk, its horn braying, its brakes squawking. We felt we were sure to kill one of these unhappy people, and what made this conviction horrible beyond its normal horror was the secret idea, which one could not prevent seeping into the other thoughts, that India would be better off for one person, or many persons, the fewer.

The people had not looked exactly unhappy, they were stuporous, unsmiling somnambulists at the end of the world, in the Indian dust, in the heat. This is how the end of the world will be, I thought. It will be tired and hopeless, without anger—it will just run down. The end of the world is beginning here. At this thought, something of their apathy affected me too, so that I had dreaded coming to India, fearing to view the vaunted suffering, the poverty, the corpses glimpsed by the side of the road, the grisly cremations along the Ganges (suttee perhaps! and the victimized child-widows, prostituted and thrown out—I had read about all the horrors of India and had feared to see them), but now here was only this methodical and slow progress of all India along the road to Agra, without hope, and since there was no hope of helping or changing it—that was apparent at a glance—I found it hard, in a way, to care any more than they did.

Even J., who was seldom apathetic, seemed in the heat a little stunned and quiet. We stopped at a rest station for tourists—a spruce, well-maintained place, with toilets. On the plane I had talked with a young Peace Corps kid, a boy from Washington, who had said, "They refuse to use toilets! They want to keep shitting in the fields! They take the money for sanitation but then they don't use it. They like India the way it is and will never change." His voice had been full of passionate hate, outrage, that India should be like this.

Then the car had broken down. Mr. Shankar, the breast pocket of his shirt filled with tiny coins and dirty little paper bills, alms, which he distributed each time they stopped, into the flock of beggars that inevitably appeared, now emptied his pocket and seriously bargained for some help, and whatever it was was fixed by dark boys who possessed among them an iron bar and a loop of rubber. Then there was lunch at a restaurant in Agra. Mr. Shankar explained to us the dishes to order—the curried lamb, the *saggosht*, the *pappadams*. He himself ate chick-peas, was a vegetarian, he said. Heat and dust choked us, even inside the restaurant. Would we never see the Taj Mahal?

Then at length we had seen it—a glorious, lacy, pale building, its exquisite Moghul domes reflected in an unsullied long pool—a tranquil and otherworldly oasis in the horrid Indian countryside, more beautiful than we had imagined, but with a splendor so tomblike that it could not produce in either of us any reflections about mortal marital arrangements. Instead it made us think of death—of dead India, and of the people's complicity with the suicide of their land, and of how hard it was for us as Americans to understand what the end of the world would be like.

Night had fallen as we drove back to Delhi. The blackness was sometimes thrust back for a moment by a campfire
along the road or in a field, or by a lantern hung in an
occasional food stall, with people gathered under a canvas
tent to eat stew ladled out of a battered caldron. These
scenes bespoke a certain desperate camaraderie; outside the
range of light were always eyes, human eyes in darkness, like
the eyes of animals caught in headlights, staring at us as we
swept along each road. And as we drew nearer to the eyes,
we could see the human forms stilly huddled behind the eyes.
Then we would pass by, leaving the people squatting in the
darkness along the side of the road, hunkered down for the
night because this was where they lived, by this road, in the
ditch, and in the morning would get up and trudge along
to nowhere in particular, going somewhere else for no reason.
Thousands of people sunk in the blackness by the side of the
road.

"What happens in the winter? Is it cold?" J. asked Mr.
Shankar.

"It can be cold, but then that is very bad because the
people die, and also when it is very hot they die."

"There are too many people," I said. I heard Mr. Shankar's
sigh.

"They have so little pleasure in life," he said, as if to
forestall a familiar discussion, Westerners always going on
about birth control.

Then we had driven down the detour road toward the office
of the nephew of Mr. Shankar's brother-in-law, and Mr.
Shankar had disappeared into the night, reappearing with a
bottle of wine, and had given it to us. Even more than in
Guatemala we had been stricken with shame, after the day
and the things we had seen, to be responsible for needing
this, for having asked for anything, and God knew what it

had cost Mr. Shankar, money that he might otherwise have given in alms.

And then, inevitably, the bottle had been broken. Cradled on the seat beside us, tended carefully, nonetheless it had slipped down and been battered by a loose spring—we had hit a bump and heard the sickening crack of the bottle. Mr. Shankar had said, gravely, at the end of the journey as we apologized and grieved, "It is of no moment. It was not meant that it should be drunk. But I am sorry that now you will have no wine." As though it were not our fault. Then he had refused to dine with us, had to return home, he said, bowing, making the little steeple with his hands. J. and I showered in our room, and ordered wine in the hotel dining room without problem.

And we had hated Ravi's uncle, in the perverse way of things, for his kindness to us and because we had broken his gift. The sedulous hospitality of Asians had an underside, I thought. It made a claim on you that the tactful European reticence we are accustomed to does not. Perhaps that was the Asian idea, that by knowing what hardships your host was putting himself to, you gave yourself into his power.

With the satisfaction of not having been behind the mischief of the Chateau Talbot 1982, I sipped at my tiny portion. It tasted weak and warm next to the powerful peanutty chili taste of the morsels of pork, the banana fritters, and fish balls coming around, the leaf-wrapped parcels of perfumed rice, shaped like the tiles of the palace roof—Thai sumptuousness, commanded by Mr. Kagura, and approved or disapproved by Mrs. Prangithornbupu, who nodded with a smile at the waiters, or gave the tiniest quizzical frown, at a lacquer platter of lemon-smelling grass.

All at once, another swarm of waiters, like a fife and drum

corps in their gold braid and smart bellboy hats, circled the table, smiling, all carrying bottles of red wine. The set, worldly, watchful expression of Mr. Kagura gave no indication of his emotions as he directed the expensive, the ruinous, uncorking of six new bottles. It seemed to me that Mrs. Prangithornbupu relaxed, some moment of national disgrace had passed and abundance reigned. More dishes followed. The face of Dr. Kora, across from me, was beautifully red. I had seen this reddening of the face before in Japan, among men in the hotel lobby bar, as they loosened their ties and began laughing, and once when we had been taken to a geisha dinner, and the solemn doctors of the afternoon had turned before our eyes into laughing, ruby revelers and had made me wonder what the reason was for the redness, something physiological, maybe. But now I felt my own face to be red, too, maybe from the chili, since it could not be from such a tiny amount of wine.

I was talking again, or rather listening, to Mrs. Kagura: "Learn Thai, shop, play tennis when it isn't too hot, which is almost always." *Arways.* Despite her excellent English, small mistakes had crept into her *r*'s and *l*'s. "My husband gone a lot—he has the whole Pacific to dear with. I would like to have a Japanese cook, with the Thai, the food is good but so spicy. But you can't get a Japanese to come out. We brought our amah, but she went back within four month." Her words became more rapid, and harder to understand, and, when I looked more closely, I could see that the delicate paleness of Mrs. Kagura's cheeks had deepened to plum.

There was also, in her voice, a louder note, which caused Mr. Kagura too to glance across the table at his wife. Her face seemed to shine. She was smiling with extra gaiety. Symptoms of drink? All at once, she gripped my hand. The soft, pretty fingers, with their impressive jewels, clamped with considerable force on my hand—now, to my own eyes, freckled, wizened, badly manicured, a hand that until tonight I had taken for granted.

"I am not feeling too well," said Mrs. Kagura. "Could I perhaps ask you to accompany me?"

"Where? Yes, of course," I exclaimed, leaping up. Mrs. Kagura also rose, holding heavily onto my arm. She smiled at her husband, whose expressionless notice revealed, to me at least, his surprise and displeasure. Mrs. Kagura, with her free hand, swooped down upon her wineglass, hoisted it like a Viking, offered a gesture of toast to her husband and table. "Ha! ha! ha!" she laughed, like Traviata in the opera. Not like Butterfly.

She set the wineglass down with only a tiny splash, though I had anticipated a spreading stain of red across the pink tablecloth. This made me remember another wine experience, in France, when I had been more or less in the position of Mrs. Kagura, in the grandeur of a sumptuous restaurant. It had not even been I who had spilled the wine, it had been, now that I thought of it, Don Harmon, who with his elbow had knocked over my glass, of a wine so elegant, revered, and expensive that the French people had gasped with horror, masking this in seconds with polite gaiety. An entire glassful, soaking the white damask from one side to the other of the table.

"When the waiter comes, you just say, *'Désolée, j'ai fait une petite tache,'*" someone instructed me, and, when I said it, the French all whooped with laughter to watch the perfection of the waiter's unruffled demeanor at this colossal understatement.

Mrs. Kagura had made only a little stain. We moved toward the ladies' room, Mrs. Kagura giggling softly, and, when we got there, she was immediately sick, making large stentorian retching sounds, and gasps of agony. I wet a towel and handed it into the toilet stall for her to sponge her forehead with, and wipe her mouth. Though I have few instincts toward medicine and healing, I felt sorry for the Japanese woman, and, remembering a few times in college when I myself had thrown up in fraternity house toilets or at the side of the road, remembered also that cold towels were comforting.

"I am so sorry," said Mrs. Kagura, when she was able to come out and splash her face at the sink, washing away the tears of retching and shame on her cheeks. "It was the wine. I am not used to it. My husband is furious."

I tried to assure her that nothing had been noticed. What on earth could he be furious about? Mrs. Kagura had after all made only a little stain, and committed only the little sin of speaking loudly. She would get scolded by her husband this time, but she'd get used to drinking wine too. Wasn't the world going to belong to these people? I liked her better now, and forgave her the business about the ring.

I said reassuring things like, "You look perfect, no one will have any idea you weren't feeling well. It was probably the food. This Thai food is hard to digest, I definitely agree. Are you ready to go back? What is your first name?"

"Kiko," said Mrs. Kagura. "My husband is furious. Japanese women do not go out in the evening, you know. It's a man's world."

When we got back to the others, the company had risen and stood in groups that moved slowly toward the doors of the dining room. There was a certain atmosphere of panic or disorder that I did not at first understand. The Western guests were all wearing expressions, variously manifested, of surprise, dismay, embarrassment, and indecision. A similar bright, fascinated, and discomfited stare transfixed their eyes. All I could at first imagine was that they had been asked to share the bill. J. walked with Dr. Prangithornbupu, whom I knew he didn't like. Dr. Prangithornbupu stood no higher than the middle of J.'s chest, and his manner was one of advantage, if not triumph, something in his smirk always managing to suggest that people of J.'s height were handicapped and bound to miss out on subjects of interest, sights, the happenings around them.

"My dear Dr. M.," he had said that afternoon at the National Museum, with an air of solicitude, "I am afraid these many Buddhas will tire you."

"Certainly not," J. had said, vigorously, though in fact the sole affliction of which he ever complains is a sore back brought on by slow walking in museums.

Kiko and I went to recover the purses we had left on our chairs. Normally Dr. Prangithornbupu said nothing at all to me, but now he detached himself from J. and the other men and said to me, "Don't worry, Mrs. M., it is not a naughty massage."

"Massage?" I said, uncertain I'd heard correctly.

"They have a massage for the ladies too," said Dr. Prangithornbupu.

It was clear that, whatever was up, Mrs. Prangithornbupu was not joining in. "I'll say good night," she said now, extending her hand. A woman in her forties, in her sleeveless cotton shift and gold bracelets, she had the figure, and the upper arms, of a twenty-year-old.

"Massage?" I repeated. I now observed a look of bewilderment on all the Western faces, and turned to J. for explanation.

"Dr. Prangithornbupu has proposed to take us all for a massage," J. said, wearing a strange expression, of amusement but at the same time a little shocked. "But I've explained that you and I have to get back early to our hotel, on account of our early plane in the morning, and that we will take the water taxi home from here."

"Oh," I said, not knowing whether to feel disappointed at missing out on the oddness of a hosted massage party. I knew that he was thinking of something we had seen on television—where? somewhere in Europe, late at night, in a hotel room, a sort of porn travelogue about Thailand. "Yes, we're getting up early," I said to Dr. Prangithornbupu, though I doubted he was offering his guests a pornographic massage. Surely there were other kinds in Thailand?

"Yes, I have to get back too," said Dr. Carole Black of Australia, anxiously coming to stand next to us.

"Yes, yes, I *aussi*," cried Dr. Narcisse Cosset, the great Parisian physiologist, and these two scrambled after J. and me with the air of people escaping a flood. We repeated our thanks, our good-byes. Dr. Prangithornbupu, his expression wounded and puzzled by the hysterical defection of these peculiar Westerners, extended his soft little hand, then turned to the other guests. Some of these also, menaced by the reputation of sexy Thai massage parlors, or by the defection of J. and the other famous professors, were beginning to launch apologies and excuses. "Good night," said Dr. Randy Deckhorne, the English surgeon. I wondered whether Don Harmon would go with Dr. Prangithornbupu or return to the hotel. I could not see him among the knot of Asians who moved with Dr. Prangithornbupu toward the hotel entrance. There, Mrs. Kagura stood waiting for a taxi with Mrs. Prangithornbupu.

On the Chao Phraya River, the sounds of Bangkok, even at this hour, like an echo in a canyon, rose behind us. The air was pleasantly scented with oil and pepper. Ahead, we could see the pier of the Oriental Hotel strung with lanterns. I thought about how it was the Westerners who had fled the after-dinner outing—Canadians, Australians, Americans, the Englishman, Dr. Randy Deckhorne, and the Frenchman, Dr. Cosset. Why? What was the objection to this unconventional way of winding up the evening? To going en masse? The hour? Surely under ordinary circumstances J. would consent to have his back rubbed, as well as other parts of him. Was it the reputation of Bangkok masseuses, or each other's company that exercised this strange censorship? What was the connection with wine? I began to feel I would rather have liked to have my back rubbed after dinner.

"Did the Japanese go?" I asked. "What about Dr. Lum? Why didn't you want to go? Were you embarrassed?"

"Me? No, it was just that I couldn't stand the idea of going across Bangkok in a taxi yet again. It takes two hours to go a mile, even at this hour. Those poor bastards, Harmon and the others—they won't get to bed before three." J. spoke with a passion surprising from someone who had had a good dinner. "I'll give you a back rub in the hotel, if you like," he added.

We stopped in the Oriental's bar and had a gin and tonic before we went up, and talked over the dinner party.

"Seven bottles of Chateau Talbot in Bangkok. Imagine what that cost. Poor Kagura must be reeling." J. laughed.

"It was really bad of Don Harmon to do that," I agreed.

"You know, D., it was bad of you to take some," J. said.

"I know, but I wanted some," I said. What a prig J. is! I felt, all at once, angry with him, impatient. How tiresomely cautious he was. Why not have gone to the Thai massage parlor? How unlike he and I were, and how unsuited, really. Why shouldn't I have had a sip of wine? I said this to J., my quarrelsome mood catching him by surprise, but he wouldn't quarrel. He laughed and asked if I remembered the television film.

The television film was clear in our minds. A pretty Thai woman in a bathing suit approaches a man lying on a beach. She speaks, he nods, the voice-over explains that this tourist is going to experience a wonderful Thai specialty.

Now the man is lying on his stomach, naked, on a comfortable-looking bed in a pretty hotel room. Through the partly open blinds, a scene of surf and blue sky beyond. The man's face, turned on the pillow, is wearing an expression both wary and committed. The masseuse is taking off her bathing suit. Now, naked, she pours a flacon of oil over her arms and stomach and spreads it between her legs. She is so slim she is almost like a child, with only tiny spots for nipples; but her expression is impassively of a grown female working at a job. She pours oil on the man's back, and on his calves, and spreads it around.

Now she climbs astride his peaceful back and begins to slither her vagina along his spine. Her thighs grip his shoulders, arms, waist, while her cunt does its work of pressing and wild rubbing and gymnastic sliding. Faster and faster over his arms, neck, upper legs. Now she flips him over and begins on his front side. Her flowerlike face has a professional expression of fixed cheerfulness. J. wonders what all this must feel like. I wonder what it must feel like to do it. The camera angle edits out a sexual climax, which seems to arise from whatever she is doing to his lower body. The camera focuses on the man's expression of dreamy satisfaction, with the girl off camera, the top of her head occasionally popping into view as she works below.

However these images might have affected our mood we were not to learn. Almost the moment we were back in our hotel room, we were startled by loud knocking on the door. Like a bride, J. shrank beneath the sheets, and I shot into the bathroom for a robe. At the door were two tiny Thai women. From their young and slender bodies, I at first thought they must be proper Thai masseuses, perhaps arranged by Dr. Prangithornbupu, or hookers prowling the corridors of the hotel. My incomprehension must have shown on my face, for they bowed and giggled, and took from a paper sack the basted shells of the silk suit and blouse I had ordered that afternoon at an atelier near the hotel—an address I had got from Huguette Cosset.

"We have come for your fitting, madame," said the one who now looked familiar. "You said you would see us at eleven-thirty." I had meant eleven-thirty the following day, of course, but they were used in Thailand to working around the clock, finishing things in a day or two for people who had to catch planes. Hand in hand the two little women came in, like lovely dolls, and hung me about with threads and collar pieces. I thought of the shoemaker and the elves. When they had gone, I climbed wakefully into bed beside J., but he had gone to sleep, wearing a slightly disappointed expression, leaving me to toss restlessly and fret at the calls of the boatmen pushing out to the early-morning markets in the klongs.

The Wildebeest

The great migration of the wildebeest, or brindled gnu (the white-tailed gnu being now almost extinct and found only in zoos), begins in central Tanzania in the middle of May, when the animals have depleted the grasses of the plains and need to set off for the higher ground and fresher pastures around Lake Victoria, in southern Kenya. More than a million does, bucks, and six-month calves, born after the return last season, travel more than a thousand miles, pausing in the patches of fresh grass, and stampeding across the rocky deserts, across rivers and the copses of thorn tree, trampling any who fall, and leaving behind any who falter—the weak, exhausted animals, the old, and the young who lose their mothers, for the others will not succor them. These stragglers are then prey to lions, cheetahs, and hyenas, who slink along behind the herd and teach their cubs the art of killing—killing for mere practice now, because they cannot eat all that they kill. Behind the cats follow the jackals, the hunting dogs, and finally the storks and buzzards picking at the bits of carrion, and rooting in the brush, where severed ribs have been dragged by the jealous predators to gnaw in solitude. The whole process is surprisingly swift, from the moment the jaws of the cat clamp the neck of the terrified, whinnying animal, its skinny legs kicking ineffectually, until it lies like a pile of ignominious sticks, long strips of hide ripped off its flanks, the whole a pile of neatly desiccating bones in half an hour.

The television documentary we had seen in the lodge at Arusha had dwelt unfairly, I felt, on these examples of the operation of pitiless nature on the slow, the weak, the small, and the unlucky, for now I saw that many gnus were going to survive, too, and the vitality in the hooves was reassuring, gnus galloping across history, if not the one, the many.

Individual dramas of life and death were not visible from the peak where we stood with the rest of the party, at a safe remove above the herd, which had begun to roll below us on the plain like a mass of swelling black lava, an intact wave in which each separate animal could barely be discerned, hidden in the cloud of dust sent up by the four million hooves, and the shimmer of the shining gray-brown of the flanks of the big creatures coursing northward at heedless speed, as if in some desperate panic at an unseen goad. The leaders were already out of sight over the horizon, and the animals that pounded by directly below us were only the middle of the herd, whose end could not be seen.

With me were J.; Maren Sorengaard, a Danish woman who made documentary films; and a young French doctor, Sylvie Brounard, who worked with the World Health Organization; together with our driver, camp attendants, and the guide, Ridu Palengo. Each was in Tanzania for his own reasons, but we had fallen in together for the expertise of Ridu and the other Africans and the use of the long-bed German truck and Land Rovers belonging to Safari Tours, which could take us and our equipment into rough country to see animals and reach the remote villages of the Masai. Some nights we made camp, and sometimes we stayed in one of the surprisingly luxurious lodges that stick up out of the flat Serengeti among outcroppings of rock. These are run by the Marxist and puritanical government of Tanzania as best it knows how, to a standard of decadent international comfort, four-course dinners with entremets, and fish knives.

"There are too many of the wildebeest," the Dane, Maren, said, in her dogmatic way, her speech as sonorous as the commentary of her films. "When man upsets the balance of nature, he makes a mess of it, but it is the beasts who suffer." As she was large and handsome, her pronouncements carried the force of original thought.

"Man has nothing to do with this," protested Sylvie, who had disagreed with Maren on nearly every point in every discussion. "It is a question of the rain. When there is plenty of rain, the animals multiply; when it is a dry year, they die off, their numbers controlled by the food supply."

"When the Masai were allowed to live as they were meant to, they controlled the numbers of the wildebeest." Their argument about man and nature had arisen from the moment the two women had met, and it was as if the dislike they felt for each other went deeper than these arguments warranted, the antipathy of two species. One was stout, the other slender, like the hippo and the lion. They had met earlier in the month, before the arrival of J. and me, when the truck party was assembled at Lake Manyara, and had continued with increasing rancor, as if each had begun to suspect that the other was entirely responsible for, respectively, the callous neglect or the benign but disastrous interference that had intensified the woes of this beautiful country. The pink-cheeked Danish woman was making a film about the Masai, and the World Health Organization doctor was making a study to understand the strange anemia that caused Tanzanian babies to die in numbers.

Compared with them, I felt frivolous, was there to look at animals and maybe buy some handicrafts at Lake Manyara, where there was a little settlement and the local traders sold beadwork belts, and the long earrings worn by Masai men, and watches with beaded dials and no works, and skirts of hide, perfect for California wall ornaments. One would want nothing to do with the appalling ebony figurines, each uglier than the last, or the pitiful little hairy drums or bark wall plaques or cowbells on strings. It seemed to me that Tanzania needs a crafts advisor, someone who could help them get the materials they need, and a fair price. The department stores in Paris or San Francisco mark up the beaded belts ten times over.

"Have you got something else to trade, mother?" the traders had asked. I had brought calculators and perfume, but they wanted more—everything. "I'll give you something for your hat," they said, "your shoes," for such was their desire for any material object at all, and when I pointed out that my feet were the wrong size, it made no difference. I gave away my plastic water bottle. Tanzania is preplastic and still uses lovely objects of straw or tin.

"Would you want ivory, missus?" they whispered, causing me to remonstrate and scold, furious at their lack of understanding. "Certainly not! How horrible! Don't you understand about the ivory trade? When the animals are dead no one will come here. Don't you understand?"

But it seemed they do not. "This one, mother, this one not ivory, no fear, no—this one made from teeth of hippopotamus." The penalty for someone caught selling ivory is immediate jail, and a long sentence, for at least the government, if not the people, believes that wildlife is the key to the country's future.

J. had been working with the International Infectious Disease Council, in Dar es Salaam, on some studies of AIDS. When he arrived in Arusha, he described conditions of unutterable misery, a hospital without aspirin or insulin, where the AIDS patients two to a mattress were left to die on camp beds that were pierced so that the incurable diarrhea could drool into buckets beneath without bothering anyone—there was no one to bother, just the old man who came now and then to take away the buckets. No one knew who these people were, tribesmen far from their villages and families, who had left them to die without naming them, black skeletons unable to murmur or lift their hands. His voice would catch, talking about this. There was nothing to be done—it was that he couldn't stand—a vigorous person used to making a difference. I was glad he was taking a few days off to look at animals in the bush, in the calm of nature, for he was strained and morose. A friend of ours, Edward Howar, had written a novel about Africa, which he said no one wanted to read, "because no one cares about Africa. They hate it. It is unreal to them, strange, dark people with stretched lips, jungle, bugs." But it was real to J.

"Africa defeats everyone," people told us, almost cheerfully. Even Africans said with apparent indifference to the present anguish, "Africa will endure," and some old friends from the English foreign service had abbreviated the whole idea of hopeless to one word, WAWA, which meant West Africa Wins Again, over any attempt to explain or improve it. East Africa was like this too.

That was perhaps the reason that the Africans had not seemed eager to be helpful to Sylvie at her task of drawing the blood of one hundred men, women, and children, randomly selected, in each of several villages of the Lake Manyara and Serengeti region. For several days one or another went along with her to the little houses of the villages to carry the apparatus and translate when her Swahili was inadequate, but this was not a relished task, and the drivers and camp men laughed when it came time to do it, and each shoved the other toward the medical valises. She was going to analyze the blood for a number of diseases, and would send the people who needed care to Arusha to the hospital. When she came along for drinks with the others on the veranda of the Lake Manyara hotel, after a day of this work, she would appear exhausted but exhilarated too, and would giggle as she drank her glass of port, relaxed until the Danes came in from their day of filming, when she would reassume her air of calm scorn. Or she would flirt with the guide, Ridu, a light-skinned, handsome Meru man of forty, with some stamp of an Arab trading ancestor on his features, and in the straightness of his hair. I had noticed that their laughter, loading and unloading the trucks, had the charged brightness of sexual awareness. Sylvie was young, in her twenties, and had some of the studied wildness I associated with the French au pair girls who came to San Francisco. She wore her eye makeup no matter where, and her hips were no bigger than a ferret's.

The Danish filmmaker was firm about not wanting to photograph animals. I could understand this, was myself at first a little bored by the animals. I had seen the sophisticated, humane zoos where all had been made to look like Africa, and these had spoiled me, so that in the beginning it was hard to feel the difference, really to feel the frisson of danger and distance the sight of a wild lion, smeared with gore, eating his kill ought to bring. But now after a week I had begun to see the scale of the animals' estate, the Serengeti plains more vast than Nebraska, and I began to feel the cruelty of zoos.

In the first days, the guide, Ridu, had been able to spot things we couldn't—the twiggy necks of giraffes among the tree trunks, stumps in the tall grass that were lions, rocks that would turn out as we drew closer to be lounging, pink-muzzled hippos, smiling their crocodile smiles—a vast inanimate world of grass and scrub acacia with its menacing thorns contained in their various disguises a huge population of stalking, grazing, lurking, wandering creatures, all apparently indifferent to Land Rovers and trucks.

It is J. who is always falling in love with a traveling companion, a star in a film, an urchin, a village bride, and, now, I could see he was smitten by Ridu, for being intelligent and informed, and manly against all the odds of Africa, and for sharing his enthusiasm for birds. The bird book *The Birds of East Africa* lay on the front seat of the Land Rover between them; their two pairs of binoculars bounced on their chests as they traced with their forefingers the trajectory of a sudden bird starting across the sky. J. was already trying to think how he could help the man—send books to his children, perhaps, and make sure to praise him to the outfitters of Safari Tours—these last were three American brothers, the sons of a Lutheran minister, who had stayed on after independence like pioneers in a movie, with their German wives, their stockade, their array of wagons and carts and trucks and earthmoving tractors, their rugged good looks, jeans, and wide hats.

I was glad we had a Tanzanian guide rather than one of the brothers, since you can always talk to Americans in America. In a certain way, it might be America just here, on the high Montana range, maybe, or on one of those grassy north ern California meadows that lie between the sea and the coastal range. Here in Africa were the same plants, moistened by the perennial mists; here it was more beautiful, unmarred by telephone wires or road signs, and the only people were the gaunt, beautiful Masai children in their purple robes, carrying staves, urging their little cows along the road. "Don't look at them, don't take their pictures," Ridu said of their fancifully painted faces. "They only do it to get money. It's bad that they should learn to depend on such a way of making money, then they don't want to work." He was puritanically proud of Tanzania, and often read in a book called *Honest to My Country*, by "Candid Scope," which held that the rigid communism taught by Nyerere, the nation's idealistic Marxist leader, had been too rigid for economic survival. "Let us be guarded against 'fashionable' socialists, opportunists, hypocrites, ideological parrots and flatterers. Such characters are great enemies of our people. At this stage in our history we should not be trying to blame particular groups or individuals for things which are not to our liking, nor not to the liking of the people," an idea that I supposed assuaged his socialist conscience about encouraging white people and tourism.

Ridu was friendly but professional, so it was only gradually that he confided the details of his life and family. He had five children, four boys and a girl. "I like gells," he said, apologizing for having so many children. "I know that the biggest problem in Tanzania is the birth control, that I know. My wife has a soft spot for the sons. But I was always hoping for another gell. How many children do you have?"

"Four," I put in, quickly, speaking for both of us, just as J. was about to explain that I had four and that he had three others. This confuses foreigners. When I say that we have seven, I must quickly add, to deflect their undeserved congratulations, that I am not the mother of all of them. Then they understand perfectly. We were sitting by the campfire, but the sky was still light enough to read by. We had the newspapers from Arusha.

"Read this," said Ridu. "In the guesthouses, the AIDS posters have been taken down. The hosts take down the posters, or the women take them down, they don't want the guests to find out the dangers. They don't believe the dangers. A man sees a woman, he thinks, that one, she looks nice, there can't be anything the matter with her."

J. took the paper and read the article, shaking his head and exclaiming, "Awful, what are they thinking of! What's the matter with people!" All human frailty constantly shocks him; instances of ignorance and perfidy always take him by surprise.

Everywhere we saw the brightly draped Masai women with tall baskets on their heads, sliding along, babies tied in kanga cloths on their backs, or tied to the backs of the little girls of four or five who walked beside them. Sometimes the women put their hands over their eyes as the Land Rover threw a cloud of dust on them. Africa was mothers, babies, dust, biology.

"The Masai house is a very brilliant adaptation to the conditions of life on the Serengeti plain," said Maren, tossing her silky, Dutch-boy hair. "At first I admit I was shocked by the darkness. But as we sat there I came to understand how they are protected in this way from the grueling sun, and of course from the animals, even insects. You do not enter straight in, there is a kind of maze leading you to the center. When I sat with the woman in her house, in the darkness, I could see she was at ease and proud. And now the government wants to put them all in these horrors of cement block and tin. These things Americans call progress."

On her plump arm was a handsome array of the sort of bracelet I had been buying.

"Really, Tanzania is a socialist country, you can't blame the Americans," Sylvie immediately said. I had seen both the tin horrors and the real Masai houses—dusty, round-topped structures whose eaves come down to the ground, like haystacks of mud and straw, ranged in circles to pen in their little cows, whose blood they are said to drink, tapping them like maple trees.

"It is perfectly good for them, there is nothing inherently wrong with it," said Maren. "Why is it any different from blood sausage or what you French people call *au jus*?"

"They have a diet very inadequate in vitamins, essential fiber, even fats," said Sylvie, growing angry. "You have only to look at that rusty-colored hair. Really, it is people like you, who exploit these people and leave them to die!" and she abruptly left our gathering.

The antagonism between the two women was so pronounced that even Ridu, and Dick and Charlie, the driver and camp man, had begun to notice and grin at the peppery stride of the young woman as she rushed off into the brush to master herself after one of these discussions. If they were paying attention to the arguments, it was the Dane they appeared to agree with. They always saw to it she had plenty of beer, and they carried the camera equipment reverently.

We watched the gnus for some hours. Even Ridu, even Charlie and Dick, who must have seen the migration countless times, were rapt, and only when it began to get dark did we drive back to the lodge. This was the Lobo Lodge, a hotel of unimagined splendor, with walls of boulder and glass, open to the valley, which on account of its remoteness had no electricity or hot water until nightfall, when the generators began to hum, and the guests began to think of showers and drinks. Maren had arranged, after dinner, to show a video of one of her earlier documentaries, and the huge lounge was thronged with guests and staff, for whom films were a novelty.

The subject was the initiation of young girls of a Nigerian tribe, a ritual that was losing favor but was still practiced by those who wanted to hold on to the old ways, as Maren's voice-over, richly amplified, explained. Four girls of about fifteen, bare-breasted and self-conscious-looking, stood in a village square, being stared at by others and allowing their breasts to be pinched by a scrawny, peering old woman who was painted blue. The woman pronounced that they were not pregnant and could be admitted to the rite. "If the breast is soft, there is no pregnancy, if it is hard the gell will be pregnant," said the old woman to the camera.

Then the bodies of the girls were painted, by expensive specialists who understood the ancient art of contriving designs that would enhance the individual beauty of each subject; circles and round shapes introduced to the skinny shoulders and breasts of the youngest an idea of voluptuousness, while the fat girl got geometrics of a slenderizing sort. An ancient art, saved up for by the parents of the girls. Now, thus ornamented, they were taken and shown off again in the square, and then their legs, from ankle to thigh, were confined in brass rings, weighted down so that the girls moved with the stately deliberation of robots. They would wear this apparatus for three weeks, during which they would stay in their houses, emerging only after dark to relieve themselves. In the house, they would eat all the time, foods as rich as their parents could afford, with the idea that to be fat is to be more marriageable and fertile. During the fattening-up period, other women would tell them old, female, things.

Next a special costume was fitted. Maren had documented each of these episodes, the morose girls gorging themselves in their huts, the old women sewing the strange costumes, like spare tires, which would be fitted in order to make the hips appear even fatter than they were, and make their buttocks like the buttocks of sows.

In their costumes, the girls sat in the square in the decorated booths and were looked at. Then they ran a race, chased by the little boys of the village, who were painted gray to look like monkeys, and by the bigger boys, leopards, and by the high priest, who hit them with his stick, to ensure they would be fertile. After the race, the girls were to be considered grown, marriageable women. "At first I was afraid the sticks would hurt me," said the skinny youngest girl.

"Yes, I am glad I did Irea," said another, to Maren's camera. "Otherwise, when I am married, my baby would die."

When the lights went back on, Sylvie snorted and shook her head, heaving French sighs of disgust. "Those poor girls, fattening them like cattle."

"I think it is not so bad," said Ridu. "It is not modern, yet it gives the gells a sense of self-worth and dignity." This made Sylvie shriek. I tended to share Sylvie's indignation, even allowing for cultural difference. Of course I knew that my own wedding ring was just an abbreviated symbol of the same condition of being chattel that the brass leg rings symbolized. "Did your daughter do Irea?" I asked Ridu.

"No," he said shortly, his face closing over.

An observation of Calvino's concerning the traveler: "The traveler recognizes the little that is his, discovering the much he has not had." In travels, I was often amazed to be brought face to face with my own lack of imagination, things I couldn't have guessed. During the projection of Maren's documentary, I had felt—I had not turned to look—that the hands of Ridu and Sylvie stirred toward each other in the dark. And now I noticed that, a few minutes after Sylvie had left, Ridu was saying good night too.

At eleven the generators would shut down and the lights would go off. The Africans—the staff, the guides and drivers, the maids and souvenir shop girls—all these began to wander off to the compound where they stayed. The guests were the last to go to their rooms. J. and Maren drank another beer at the bar, and I had a glass of wine.

"What do you think?" I asked J. "Could there be something between Sylvie and Ridu?"

"Oh, probably not," J. said. "Sylvie knows as well as anyone the seroprevalence of HIV around here. You'd have to be very, very careful if you got mixed up with an African."

As we walked Maren to her room in the dark, I thought of that other African Dane, Karen Blixen, and her European disease. In the dark we could hear the night calls, and frog noises, and feel the eyes of baboons on us from the roof and behind the pillars. The moon was coming up from behind the low hills to the east to light the nocturnal prowls of the animals waking up on the plain below and stealing out into the clearings.

We set off in the morning by early light, with a full day's itinerary—a Masai village where Maren would film and Sylvie, aided by the chivalrous J., would do her medical work, then to the Olduvai Gorge, where Leakey, the English paleontologist, had discovered the oldest human bones; wildlife and birds for J. along the way, and perhaps another encounter with the wildebeest herd.

Ridu, in a good humor, entertained us with the story of a friend of his. "My friend has nineteen children." He laughed. "The fool. Birth control is our biggest problem in my country. Still, he is worse than most. His first wife had twin gells, then another pair of twin gells and then—what do you know! Another pair of twin gells, and then another one gell. So my friend got another wife, telling me, I can't get sons from that one. But the next wife produced only gells. I knew her, she was one from my village. All right, now he has thirteen gells, and he gets a third wife, and from her, six, also gells. And, when I last saw him, he told me all this, and he said he was looking for a fourth wife! 'You fool,' I told him. 'It's YOU that makes them gells!' He should have known that, he has a degree in fisheries. I knew it is the man, because one of my guests, a scientist, told me about that. Years ago. But it is also true that in this job I am in a position to find out information that others do not have, so perhaps I should be more understanding to him."

"Did he believe you?" I asked. I sympathized with him being in a place where you couldn't find out things. We came, after all, from a place where all knowledge is at your elbow, intruding on your brain, you can't keep it out. Tanzania is a country two times the size of California. There are twenty-six million people. The men live to an average of forty-nine years, the women fifty-four. Lake Victoria is the third largest lake in the world.

"Do you know what the statistical probability of a person having nineteen children of the same sex is?" said J., who had drawn out his calculator. "Wait, I'll tell you."

"Is he rich enough to feed them?" Sylvie asked.

"Yes, he is a good father, I think they all have food," said Ridu.

I expected this tale to provoke an attack from Sylvie on the heedlessness of African reproduction, or on Maren for probably being about to say that nature should bring babies as it will. Sylvie, however, screamed for Ridu to stop the car. She had noticed that several of her cases of equipment had not been loaded into the Land Rover.

"Oh, *merde, ce n'est pas vrai!* How can that happen? I put them out myself, I say to Charlie and Dick especially. Look, all we have now is cameras and film and lenses and that garbage, and my cases are not here."

Ridu stopped the car and waited for a moment while Sylvie scrambled into the back and rooted under the tarps. "See, it's true," Sylvie said. "They must have put them on the truck." The truck was headed, with Dick and Charlie, to make camp for our arrival at nightfall. Ridu got out himself, opened the back, and looked. Cameras, sound equipment, the drinks cooler, suitcases, and no medical equipment. He grimaced with chagrin.

"We better go back, in case the things are still there, sitting on the ground." He turned around. Sylvie and Maren lapsed into a silence of surly irritation, punctuated by rondos of complaint—Sylvie's that cameras should be preferred over medical supplies, Maren's for having to lose the midday light, Ridu's at the carelessness of his crew and at himself for not having overseen them. I chattered in an attempt to cheer things up, but could not escape the notion that the leaving of Sylvie's case had significance, was the projection of unconscious states, some mood that had developed among the others that J. and I did not understand. At its most obvious, it demonstrated the reluctance of Africans to deal with Sylvie's equipment, as if it were the cause, or potent symbol, of death and bad news.

"What is amazing to me," complained Sylvie, "the Dane wants them to rest in the Stone Age so she can take their pictures, and all they want is to carry her cameras to help her."

"It is absolutely stupid for us to go back, the men will have taken the things on the truck, Sylvie can do her work tomorrow," said Maren again. "Now we will lose the light in the Ngorongoro, and she won't have time to do whatever it is she does anyhow, so we will all lose a day."

The cases were not at the hotel, so they had to be on the truck. Now, behind schedule, Ridu decided to take a shortcut off the main road, across country. We drove eastward along the main road for fourteen miles, then turned off into the open plain. One sensed a new, serious sound to the engine of the Land Rover, a sort of pleasure in doing what it was supposed to do. I discerned a faint, an almost imaginary track, a mere depression in the grass as we followed along. Nothing at all on either hand, no object, sign, animal, not even a tree, just waving brown grasses, the lovely gray-gold that Karen Blixen had written about, and a vast sky. In an hour we stopped to look at a distant antelope running from us out of sight over the rise. Ridu was excited—"I'm almost sure it is a roan antelope. Now you have seen a rare animal! They are never seen around here." But to me it only looked, at this distance, much like other antelopes, graceful, shy, and fast.

After a few miles more we saw another Land Rover, parked at the top of a mesa. Ridu drove toward it over the ruts of an eroded slope, steering clear of the dugouts of hunting dogs, who poked their big ears up at the sound. In the nearby scrub were the bleaching bones of their dinners. The occupant of the Land Rover was an Englishwoman who said she was working on cheetahs. Somewhere ahead, where we could not see, was a cheetah female, pregnant and due to give birth. "Basically we're trying to learn why the cheetahs do so poorly," said the woman, with surprising resignation. "Only two in a hundred survive, though that is enough to maintain the present population. But there are too few cheetahs altogether."

"There is a roan out there," Ridu told her.

"Really?" She swung her binoculars across the horizon.

After another hour of the jolting, taciturn journey along the grassy track, Ridu called our attention to a big male lion at the job of eating his kill. He lay on the open ground in low grass. He was its same color. Ridu drove slowly toward him, and the lion did not seem to notice. "Animals don't mind Land Rovers," he said, "and they can't smell the humans inside." I could not have imagined that the lion would be so dainty, had stacked the four little hooves and forelegs with the head and the liver in a pile while he demolished the ribs and haunches. What would he leave for the hyenas and jackals and storks and buzzards waiting in their order for their turns like the children of a schoolyard—the bullies, the timid, the aloof? I was not surprised that his maw wasn't bloody, so daintily did he eat. I took pictures of him with my Minox. From time to time he looked menacingly at the carrion eaters, lest they come too close too soon.

"The lion has a civilization like the American civilization," said Ridu, "a society where everyone defends his rights. In Africa, we are gentler, we tend to say, 'Well, he is older than me, let him sit down first, let him have my bit of meat.' "

All at once the Land Rover came to a halt with a clank. At first I thought this was another intentional stop and waited with the others for Ridu's explanation. But from his cursing it was soon evident that this was a breakdown. One of the laws of travel is that there must always be a breakdown—there is even something reassuring about it, some assertion of natural law reminding that the world is in order. I've broken down in India, in China, in Queens, in Oregon, in France. One of my earliest memories is of my father cursing and kicking a flat tire—the only violence I had ever seen from that amiable man.

The problem was pronounced to be an accelerator cable. I climbed out, the better to enjoy the romantic situation of being broken down on the Tanzanian plain, off road and seventy miles from anyone but the cheetah woman, as nearest neighbor a lion who could still plainly be seen behind us at his placid dinner. Sylvie and Maren climbed out with me. Only Ridu and the big Danish woman looked in place here, Maren with her khaki vest and camera bag, and her lion's mane hair.

"I suppose it doesn't matter, I had completely abandoned the idea of a day's work, it's hopeless," she said.

I had brought knitting, a paperback book, and the notebook in which I kept a list of the animals we had seen: dik-dik, eland, waterbuck, warthog, hyena, elephant, wild dog, topi, crocodile, impala, cheetah, hyrax (rock and tree), black-faced vervet monkey, Cape buffalo, black rhinoceros, common zebra, hippopotamus, olive baboon, golden jackal, silver-backed jackal, banded mongoose, wildebeest, Coke's hartebeest, Grant's gazelle, Thomson's gazelle, monitor lizard, leopard tortoise, klipspringer, oryx, squirrel. To this I now added roan antelope and lion.

Maren had also given me a list of useful travel accessories, which I always carry now, and have used surprisingly often:

Band-Aids
Bendel's clear plastic zip
   compartments
black marker
candles
flashlight
moleskin
needle-nosed pliers
razor blades
recorker
small down pillow
sun cream
tape
travel mirror
tube detergent
watercolors
zip Baggies

paper clips
fishing vest
extra batteries
radio
binoculars
bungee cord
rubber bands
staples
camera and film
plastic bottle
ruler
cord
string
matches and a cigarette
carabiner
Swiss army knife
sewing kit

I turned to my paperback, half-hoping that the car could not be fixed for a while. The source of this hope was something to do with the wish that things would be more even between us and Tanzania, and between us and the animals. I could almost understand, though of course not forgive, the white hunters, or Ernest Hemingway, say, for tracking animals; for if you went after them on foot there was something equal in the contest between you, and as it was there was not, it was just you in a Land Rover, and an indifferent animal letting you watch him. You might be in the San Diego Zoo.

But to be stuck on the plains of Tanzania, let us say until night, or even until morning, when someone would miss us, and someone else hear on the radio, and the cheetah project woman report having seen us—that would be adventure. We would sleep in the Land Rover, taking turns standing guard, and there was plenty of water in the drinks cooler.

Over the clanking and disassembling, I listened to Ridu confiding to J. something he had not told the others about his family. I did not hear the beginning, only Ridu saying, "No, she will not finish school. I was disappointed in my daughter. I went all the way to Nairobi for her schoolbooks. I spent all my Kenyan money, on the books and the uniform, but then the gell and her mother told me she was going to have a baby. It broke my heart. She is not an ignorant village gell, they have classes in the Lutheran church where they tell them things, no, there was no excuse. But my wife was happy, for when the baby came, he was a boy, what she prefers."

"But why can't she finish school?" I heard J. ask. "Couldn't she go away to school?"

"I had hoped her to be a teacher," said Ridu, "but now her life is over. My only daughter, only fifteen," rejecting one after another of the optimistic J.'s suggestions. "Perhaps I will put her in a trade, perhaps to learn sewing." The finality of this Dickensian resolution appalled me too, but I did not enter into the talk. Instead, I read, half-drowsing in the sun. I heard J. say, "Here, hold it, then I'll twist it."

Then I heard Maren's cry, "That stupid girl!" and Ridu was dashing off through the grass. Looking up, we could see what he and Maren had seen, that Sylvie had wandered off from the car and was walking, rather as in a trance, slowly but intentionally toward the lion, as if she meant to march up to him and snatch his jawbone feast. I stood up to see better. J. dashed past me after Ridu, and I called out to him to be careful.

"What the hell is she doing?" Maren asked, climbing into

the Land Rover to stand up through the roof for a better look. I clambered after her.

Sylvie had stopped. She was perhaps ten yards from the lion. The scale of the big lion head and Sylvie's head seemed in the correct relation if they were near each other. Her turquoise T-shirt was the only spot of color in the dun-gold landscape. At first the lion did not appear to hear or smell Sylvie, and continued to eat. She approached a few more steps, stopped again; Ridu stopped a few yards behind her, and J. behind him, everyone waiting to see what she was going to do. We could not hear what Ridu said to Sylvie. We saw her lift her camera. We saw J. look round at us, as if to make sure that we were safe.

"Stupid girl," said Maren, looking through the viewfinder of her still camera. "Get her out of there."

Now the lion got to his feet, turned slightly, and faced Sylvie, staring gravely. I could imagine the baleful expression of his light lion eyes, for they had looked into mine while we had watched him eating. I heard the click of Maren's camera. Was it possible we were now going to see a woman attacked by a lion? Interest, rather than horror, held us. Then I saw Ridu stalk Sylvie from behind, as if she were the quarry, grab her by the shoulders, and pull her slowly backward, as away from a window ledge. He did not turn his head from the lion but stared into his eyes.

When they had retreated some yards, it appeared—I could not be sure—that Ridu struck Sylvie, cuffed her like a child. Yet, when they came up, Sylvie was smiling and excited, almost babbling, the words tumbling out in French and English. "I wanted to see what it would be like to be on foot on the plain. I imagined what if we had to walk back to the hotel! There you are walking on foot, you are just the same size as the animals, there is nowhere to hide. You are smaller!

But you are more clever. But you are not armed. See? I wasn't going any closer, *mais non!* Of course not, anyway what do you care?"

I observed a glance pass between Maren and Ridu. What it communicated I could not have said—a glance of almost connubial understanding, or parental concern, a glance of complicity. A glance in any case that testified to a history, an agenda, things unknown to J. and me, that had passed among Maren, Sylvie, and Ridu.

"Get in," Ridu told us all, as if he wouldn't trust us, and after a second of defiance Sylvie too climbed back in the Land Rover. Ridu began to call on his radio for someone from Safari Tours to bring us an accelerator cable.

Becalmed, we sat in the wilderness. Now we became aware that Sylvie, in the seat behind, had begun to sob, trying to be quiet about it, though this was impossible in such a tiny space. She sobbed at length, with her chin tucked into the front of her shirt, as if to hide the tears, which ran quite plainly down her face. Some passion was being expressed, some program followed. This peculiar event had a history, would have a future, and I had no idea what it was.

The others ignored Sylvie's sobs, whether from indifference or politeness I could not tell. I would have spoken, to say "there, there," or to ask if I could help, but I hesitated to intrude, and in a way could understand how something reckless and defiant had caused Sylvie to approach a lion, and that now, after the fact, she was scared to tears, or indignant at the manner of her rescue.

Ridu spoke again on the Land Rover's radio, in Swahili, in urgent syllables we couldn't understand. J. stared through the binoculars at the horizon, for birds, or the approach of another vehicle. Maren passed the time with the straps and lenses and dials of her equipment, all ignoring Sylvie, yet, in the cases of Ridu and Maren, with the air of knowing, or understanding, of there having been some prologue to Sylvie's behavior, or in the expectation of some aftermath, discussion of which was deferred.

My spirit refused the effort of understanding. What is the traveler except a stranger? It came to me that I could not and was not expected to understand, and that this was the lot of the traveler, to pass through, unaware of the history, ignorant of the future. Usually I mind that; it is one of the things I have against travel; but now it also came to me that this was a privileged situation, the foreigner's absolution, to see but not to understand, except what you have yourself brought with you, the things lying on your heart all along.

And there is something catching about someone crying. Sylvie's sobs made me feel sad, not for myself or even for Sylvie but for Ridu's daughter and for the whole burdened world. And less for the human world than for the animals, who less deserved their suffering.

With the end of the afternoon, we saw there was a bit of luck in finding ourselves broken down just here, for here the flanks of the wildebeest herd, or the outriders, had begun to move in, to graze and pass the night. Groups of beasts on every hand strolled over the horizon, until we were in the very midst of wildebeest as far as we could see—great bulls who defended invisibly defined patches of grass, the restless cows and frolicking young animals. Seen up close, there was something tremendously appealing about the homely creatures, they touched us, and reanimated our feelings against the cruelty of nature. So meaningless, so pathetic, each lonely gnu trying to keep for himself a cow or two, facing down the other males, the cows with fickle self-indulgence wandering to patches of thicker grass, guarded by some other male, their female openings innocently indifferent to the bucks that circled round them as they nibbled their dinner, and the terrified calves trying to keep up with all this pacing and straying and locking of horns and circling and calling. The cries of the animals, driven by their crazy instincts, tore my heart. "We discover the animals of the plain, happy and free as God intended," Karen Blixen had written, but I had begun to feel that this was a great and fatuous error.

Here and there a lonely bull turned in frenzied circles, apart from the others, like the center of a hurricane, spinning on itself. "That is the work of the larvae of the tsetse fly. The maggots get into the inner ear of the gnu and it will spin like that until it dies," said Maren in her documentary film voice. "This is because the Tanzanian government has denied to the Masai their hereditary access to the plains, upsetting the natural balance between the demands of their cows and the gnus, causing an increase in these flies, which in turn . . ."

I could not bear to look at the doomed and lonely creature in its agony, turning in its spot until it dropped, nor at the lost calf, who would die, or the big old fellow with swollen fetlocks, who would never make it this year. So many, and yet each an individual—they were like humanity itself. I missed my own children. All the suffering of the animal world bore upon me, pressing on the spirit with the urgency of a full breast. What especially struck me was that, despite the seeming tranquillity of the early evening, it was everywhere a spectacle of anxious maternity, frantic wildebeest mothers hunting among the hoard for their own calves, and hippos and the grouse hen with her little row of chicks, and the cheetah mother, and the antelopes teaching the little stick-legged babies to run, run, run. Each animal female had a flat life of eating and roaming, feeling occasional fear but not much else, no thoughts, no desire. But none had escaped the pangs of maternal anxiety, that racking terror reserved to females, knowing that life with its jaws awaits the cub, the fawn. Above all I could not bear to look at the bereft mother wandering and crying, unable to find her calf.

Cuckoo Clock

The ice on the roads, which had melted slightly during the day, had refrozen after dark into sheets of perilous glass, slippery as if they had been oiled, and the tail end of the bus as it took the curves was skidding badly. We were afraid the whole thing would overturn. It didn't help that the driver wouldn't slow at any point, except once or twice to pick up people who shouted at him out of the blackness by the snow-banked roadside and climbed on, talking in German, laughing, seeming drunk. The driver, who might have been drunk too, chattered in a loud, slurred voice and laughed—it seemed to us inappropriately—at the lashing and swaying of his bus. The members of the party, doctors and their wives or husbands, many of them from warm climates, clung terrified to each other or to the seats. The person sitting next to me, Penny Deckhorne, clung with one hand to the thin chrome rim of the bus window, spreading her fingers along it as if to stay the lurching vehicle. J. and Sir Randy Deckhorne were sitting in front with the organizer, Dr. Schneider, to talk about some program matter. I wished one of them would walk back down the aisle to say something reassuring to the passengers.

"When we signed up for it, I thought the dinner would be at the hotel," Penny said through her teeth.

I agreed. Penny's large and heavily overcoated body fell

across me with each whiplash. "Sorry," she said each time, and I said, "Sorry," when we went the other way. I withdrew my knee from the enforced lurch of Penny against me as we swerved again.

"I'm just going to get Randy to speak to the man," said Penny, climbing over me and proceeding up the aisle, clinging to the seats as she made her way. The International Infectious Disease Council was giving a course, under the auspices of its parent, the World Health Organization, in epidemiological methods to be used in studying developing countries. Perhaps two hundred professors of medicine or chiefs of hospitals, and their spouses, had come for it to Grindelwald, Switzerland. The hours of the lectures had been arranged for those who wanted to take advantage of the pistes and alpine walks, so that the time was free from nine-thirty to four. Now we were on our way to the dinner gala and toboggan ride.

Penny's intercession made no noticeable difference. The bus continued to climb along the dark road, more slowly as it grew steeper, but still slipping and swerving. The lights of the village appeared below us like the tiny lights of Christmas trees peeking through the dark branches of the forest on either side of the road. Through the window, I could see here and there an isolated chalet, lights behind closed shutters suggesting the inhabitants cozy at their dinners. As the bus toiled at the incline, I could hear the continued little exclamations of fear and distress, and murmured conversations among the passengers, many of them Asians from warm climates, bundled unfamiliarly into winter clothes. An odor of wet wool and boots, and a faint mothball smell, permeated the bus. Penny came back and sat down.

We had thought that dinner and a toboggan ride would be a pleasant thing to do, especially for the Asians, to experience the wintry night, the frosty beauty, the preposterous fairy-tale drifts of snow. But logistically it was turning out to be more complicated than we had expected—two busloads of doctors, and miles to go. Apart from the Japanese, who skied with enthusiasm, the Asians had not seemed comfortable on the slippery streets of Grindelwald, but most had signed up for this more restful and festive-sounding dinner.

"It's much farther than I thought," I said.

"It's bloody miles," hissed Penny. "Randy says he doesn't know how far it is." I noticed that Mrs. Kora, across the aisle from us, had buried her face in her hands.

From the first, I had not felt quite at ease in this German part of Switzerland; despite the vaunted comfort of their hotels, the appearance concealed an essentially puritanical edge of discomfort; the pool in our hotel, advertised as "indoor," was nonetheless kept two degrees below a temperature that human beings could find tolerable; and the skis I had rented had proved at the top of a glacier to be completely without edges, obliging me to sideslip fearfully down more than a mile of ice field as a crevasse above us emitted frightening, strange creaks of moving snow and the menace of avalanche. In the shop windows, which I scrutinized for amusing artifacts for presents, I found only figures of unpleasant-looking little dwarves and witches, and people with twisted Brueghel faces, or displays of gleaming cutlery and sinister steel dental implements. There seemed to be nothing pink, light, luxurious, no concept of decor, the food an endless succession of veal cutlets of a midwestern plainness. Yet my children were delighted with their respective activities—ski school for the younger ones, and for the older skiing with us and dinners in the hotel restaurant, like world travelers.

Then there had been the strange events of yesterday. While

J. was at his meeting in the morning, I had set out with the children toward the bottom of the lifts, our skis on our shoulders. Around, above, the mountains were shrouded in mists rising from the warmer floor of the valley, and on every side, muffled in the cottony soft clouds, came the tinny chimes and clunks of tuneless bells. It was a sound I had heard before in summer, in the Alps, bells borne by the grazing cows on the upper slopes, their sound amplified by the strange acoustics of rock and crevasse into a sort of charming bucolic orchestra. But at this season all the cows were still snugly in their winter barns, warming the human inhabitants above their heads, if such was still the practice, insulated from the tempests by bales of hay and mounds of redolent dung.

"Listen, listen," I told the children. We stood in the street, wondering as sounds seemed to be advancing on us, like elfin marauders. Gradually we could see through the mist that people were creeping down the slopes, human beings carrying cowbells converging on the town from the peaks above. Crouching, creeping, like the conspirators in an opera, holding their cowbells aloft, clinking, ringing, sneaking down the hills, hundred of bells. As we watched, a pair of old men darted behind a Mercedes-Benz parked at the curb, crouched low behind a Citroën, and sneaked into the narrow strip between two chalets. It was as if this prosperous Swiss village, with its sumptuous fondue restaurants and giant sheds housing the enormous gears of the aerial tramways, had been taken over by bell-ringing mountain gnomes.

It was charming. I could think of nothing like this in America, people sneaking through the streets carrying bells— though Halloween might strike foreigners as odd. The richness of the world in irrational customs was not to be deplored. Merely to contemplate it was a kind of happiness: the strangeness even of old, sober Europe. One thought of the blood of Charlemagne's empire, the rich legacy of popes and janissaries and followers of Hannibal, and on the other hand our American blood thinned by a diet of turkey and all that puritan Sunday reading and the practical problems of getting the wagons from here to there, leaving no time for all the elves and mountain sprites left behind us in the Old Country. The strangeness of the world. We had a pleasant day skiing and dinner *en famille* in the village, and I was ready to forgive Switzerland its attitude to untuned ski equipment and the cold swimming pool.

When the children were in bed, J. and I went out to walk in the moonlit streets. As we strolled along, we became slowly aware that people were following us. Their footsteps on ice gave curious squeaks, synchronized with the speed of our own walking. Without speaking we slowed, quickened, slowed our steps again, to see whether it could be true that we were being followed, and in each case heard other steps behind us that stopped when we did.

But, at first, this didn't seem frightening, just odd. We were after all not in America, and so did not fear robbery or mugging; the streets of a little Swiss town are safe to walk. Yet we were Americans, and by habit looked behind us, puzzled not to see what it was that produced the echo of our own steps.

"I thought there was somebody," I said.

J. said, "Look—there is somebody." Two people stood in the shadow of a porch across from us, almost invisible. Relieved at having found an explanation, we continued. Those people had nothing to do with us. We lost sight of them, and no longer heard the steps.

Then at the corner three people leapt out from behind a

hedge to block our way. I cried out in surprise, J. grabbed my arm. One person was dressed in green clothes and wore a Ronald Reagan mask, one was dressed in an Uncle Sam costume, and one was dressed and masked like Mickey Mouse. In a sliver of frosty moonlight we could see that two of the figures were pointing guns at us.

J. shoved me behind him and bravely advanced; I screamed for him to hold still. As we watched, Uncle Sam extended his gun and pointed it at J.'s head. With chilling, excruciating deliberation he made ready to shoot. We heard the first click—perhaps the gun had misfired—then another, then a third click, a pantomime of shooting J. Then, as suddenly as they had appeared, the three figures danced away into the shadows.

Only seconds had passed, it was the briefest of encounters, yet the fear, the surge of adrenaline, the sweat now chilled us and left us limp. "Jesus," J. said. Weak-legged, we staggered into the nearest haven, a bar at the end of the street, and crumpled into a booth. I put my face in my hands and tried to quell my heart by taking deep breaths. Later I thought of Dostoevsky and the firing squad.

For minutes I felt my hands shake. I felt sick to my stomach, felt the drained, shocked feeling people have after they have been robbed or injured, the interminable seconds when you believe you are about to die, and then the absence of this powerful stimulus. J., too, I could see, had the pallor of the drowned. "They spared us when they saw we were in ski clothes, they could tell we didn't have money," we said.

"They weren't muggers," J. said. "They were assassins. It's just that we weren't the people they were looking for."

Inside the little bar, fresh geraniums, a wooden clock, loden-clad drinkers in booths. From where we sat we could see the door, which now opened, and the three assassins came in carrying their guns. We stiffened like wolves, but the other patrons seemed unconcerned. They paid no attention to the curious fact that Mickey Mouse was having a drink next to them. A man at the bar moved over onto another stool so that the three could sit together. J. and I stared. The three did not seem to notice us seated in the booth at the rear, or didn't care that we were here.

The bartender was speaking to the three, but they were ostentatiously silent. Instead they mimed, pointing silently to beer and whiskey. Soon we understood that the people were in costume, and seemed to be under some oath of silence, and that the whole thing was sufficiently ordinary as to bring no comment at all from the other Swiss people. Mickey Mouse sipped his whiskey through a straw fitted into the tiny mouth aperture of his mask, and Uncle Sam hoisted his giant beer stein for a refill. Their guns, recognizably plastic, lay on the bar.

"What I really thought was terrorists, and they were going to kill us because we were Americans," I said at last.

"Yes, I did too," J. admitted. "American paranoia. But, well, the costumes, for one thing. The costumes were American. If they'd been dressed like Heidi or William Tell, we wouldn't have been so scared. Mickey Mouse was scary. Besides, where we come from, all the guns are real."

"Doesn't every Swiss have a gun? That's something the gun nuts at home always bring up."

"They never shoot each other, though. We ought to have remembered that. But how did we know they were Swiss? They could be anything—drug-running Colombians, Syrian terrorists," J. said.

"Let's face it, we were scared because we thought they were Americans," he said.

"And because *we* were Americans. I thought they knew

we were Americans," I said. Basically we're used to thinking that everyone hates us and wants to kill us. Americans. It's an idea we have without thinking about it. We automatically expect to be the target.

We sat talking about the oddness of being an American, something you couldn't help but carry around like a brand on your forehead, attracting emotions like a lightning rod, different emotions in different places, but most of them hostile. Where might you go to be loved, where did they love Americans? When, presently, J. said, "I suppose we ought to go," his voice was still a little thinned by relief. We felt a sense of the fragility of existence, but also of the oddness of feeling for two times in mortal danger in a safe country like Switzerland, the old soul of Europe. What did this mean?

And now to feel in mortal danger again, on this demented bus. At last we slowed and stopped in front of a charming, small chalet, built in the cuckoo-clock style typical of the region, with gingerbread balconies and window boxes, steeply pitched roofs, and a barn on the ground floor where in former days the cows would spend the winter.

The prospect of warmth and dinner lifted everybody's spirits, and we trooped out of the bus with merry voices in a confusion of languages. Inside were long tables covered with checkered cloths, a forest of wineglasses glittering like the icicles that dripped from the pine trees during the day, chafing dishes positioned at each few places, and a long fondue fork by every plate. This cheering sight dispelled the last notes of criticism and discontent about the ride. I found my place at one end of the head table, with another Swiss host, Dr. Wurfel, and my French friend Huguette Cosset. J. was sitting at the other end with Narcisse Cosset and Frau Freddi

Wurfel. Through the lane of candles down the center, he appeared far away and flushed, like a character in a painting by La Tour. The flame reflecting on his glasses made his countenance as distant and unreadable as his mood of late.

"Fondue is a fabulous, delicious dish," I raved to Dr. Wurfel.

"Yah, you see, we have more than the cuckoo clock," he said. So that I would understand this reference, he added, " 'After three hundred years of democracy and peace, what do they have? The cuckoo clock.' That's Orson Welles in *The Third Man*, you know, talking of Switzerland. Don't drop your bread into the fondue, you know what that means."

"Bad luck?" asked I.

Dr. Wurfel seemed reluctant to explain.

"It means you are *au monde*," whispered Huguette. Available to the world.

As the dessert was being served, a group of Swiss at the end of the second table burst into a song whose words sounded like *Oleoyolleyoleyyolee*, followed by actual yodels—this peculiar and inimitable sound coming out of the mouths of people who before dinner had seemed rather prim and plainly dressed. Tears ran down their cheeks. I strained for the words, and now heard something like *"le Roi des Vaches."*

"Not a French song, German Swiss. They are forever singing," Huguette remarked. I nodded. Sometimes packs of young German tourists broke into songs while marching up my street in San Francisco.

"This is a song," said Dr. Wurfel, "that the Swiss guards of Louis Quatorze, in France, were forbidden to sing, for when they sang, they wept, transported by nostalgic emotion, and while weeping they would be ineffective at protecting the king."

"I don't think Americans have any equivalent songs," I

said, "except maybe 'Old Black Joe,' which is probably po-
litically incorrect, or 'The Battle Hymn of the Republic.'
Nobody ever cries at 'The Star-Spangled Banner.' "

Fondue, salad, some sort of torte, wine—lots of wine,
gratefully enjoyed by the guests for its soothing effect after
the fright of the ride. Even Mrs. Prangithornbupu drank, I
observed, quite a large glass of wine. Bottles disappeared,
were replaced, were drunk—the delicious Riesling of the
area. Next, after the schnapps and coffee, the flushed and
merry revelers were interrupted by Dr. Wurfel, who rapped
his glass and got up. "Ladies and gentlemen, our host for
this fine feast will announce some things about the toboggan
ride, which is scheduled for after dinner."

The merry, pink-cheeked proprietor, in his turtleneck with
little medals pinned to it, came to stand next to Wurfel. In
his hand he carried a child's sled. "The toboggans are outside," he said. "This is just to show you how they steer and
how they operate. They can be used by one or two people
each. The person in front steers, by moving this crossbar,
while the person behind controls the speed by means of his
feet, or the driver can do this. It's really very easy to control."
He raised the sled over his head for all to see. It looked like
what I remembered as a Flexible Flyer. It began to dawn on
me that he was saying that we would now be going out into
the icy night to slide downhill on sleds, and moreover that
this was our means of returning to our hotels, many miles
below. It seemed that our host and instructor did not immediately perceive that his silent guests were struck with
horror. I at least had thought of toboggans as large, comfortable sleighs towed by horses or tractors that would drive
us festively through the country lanes around the town. I
tried to read J.'s expression at the other end of the table, but
could not. I could see that my nearer neighbors were staring

with shocked eyes at the flimsy apparatus with which this man was suggesting they would have to regain the village of Grindelwald. "The bus will be waiting for you at the end of the course, and we would appreciate it if you would assemble there, for though it is only a short walk from there to the hotel, still we want to be sure everyone is accounted for." Now a murmur of dismay went up. Someone came to the table to speak to Dr. Wurfel. People turned to each other, gasping.

Dr. Wurfel stood up beside the host and rapped with his spoon. He spoke more loudly, as if to override the surge of tense complaint. "Of course, for those of you who may not wish to take the toboggan ride, the bus will return," he said. "Ladies and gentlemen, the bus will be coming back if there are those who do not wish the toboggan ride."

I knew immediately that I did not wish the toboggan ride. We were in an unknown Swiss forest, temperature below zero, at eleven at night. We had dined well, had drunk wine and kirschwasser. It was perhaps not too much to say that we were some of us slightly drunk. I could hardly bring myself to believe that the organizers intended that this group of doctors, many stout and elderly, or delicate island people, should go outside and hurtle into the night on these dangerous contraptions, especially all the way down to Grindelwald, many miles below us. "I don't think I'm going to do it, are you?" I asked Huguette.

"*Mais oui!* It will be very agreeable," said Huguette with a bright smile. "I adore winter sport, do not you?"

"But it must be miles down to Grindelwald, is there some sort of path? It's pitch black."

"The distance is four and one-half kilometers," the host was explaining. I thought of Bataan, of the Long March, of a photo I had seen of a woman who had died on Everest, her corpse lying unburied, beyond reach on the open snowfield, forever preserved in the icy air.

The aghast revelers were prodded outside. Those who in their relief at having survived the bus ride had drunk incautiously at the dinner now tottered slightly, their voices loud. I felt this to be my case. I wished my head clearer. Many lapsed out of English and spoke in panicky whispers in the unfamiliar languages of Asia and Eastern Europe. The moon was full, which did something to illumine the dark path that led from the chalet down the mountain into the black nighttime forest, but path was perhaps not the word, for the moon was bright enough to reveal it as a rutted track, glinting icily, rising at its edge in a slight embankment that might impede the pilot of a sled from running off into the ravine or crevasse that yawned invisibly on the downhill side. From the depth of the ruts, carved by skis or the runners of sleds, the apprehensive could reassure themselves that it would be difficult for the tiny sleds to jump the track, but it would be hard to steer too. While this diminished the possibility of falling into the abyss, it also eliminated the possibility of discretionary turns for the purpose of slowing down. The rider would be as committed as on a roller coaster, with no turning back. And it was more than just an unpleasant, scary descent down steep slopes; the rider would risk running into trees or over the embankment into one of the mountain ravines that had seemed in the daylight on the pistes so dangerously deep and rocky. Despair sealed my ears.

One would also risk running into any of the other fifty or so sedentary, tipsy, maladroit, and terrified passengers—dignified international doctors transformed unwillingly into feckless adventurers defying death with their portly bodies and bejeweled wives. Various males approached the track, studying it with deliberation, but most of the wives shrank back, drawn to the comforting light that shone through the windows of the chalet, where the waitresses could be seen clearing the remains of the feast. This differentiation of sex roles was cross-cultural, common to the Japanese and American and Thai and African and German and English wives alike, leaving only one or two Swiss women, the American woman doctors, and the sportive Huguette Cosset; these, intending to pilot their own sleds, stood along with the men gazing downhill into the perilous obscurity. National differences too were apparent. Prudent Filipinos withdrew to the bus, angrily denouncing the whole folly. I caught the eye of the Thai Dr. Prangithornbupu, who seemed to be giving me a glance of sympathy as he escorted Mrs. Prangithornbupu toward the bus. Several elderly English couples also announced in tones of indignation that they would ride down.

"Mind you, that will probably be just as dangerous," said one.

I walked over to where J. was extracting a sled from the stack.

"I think we ought to go on the bus," I said. "This is stupid."

"Stupid and perilous," he agreed somewhat grimly. An Englishman, Dr. Knight, whom I guessed to be about seventy, was also selecting a sled.

"J.," I went on, surprising myself to hear my wail, "I don't see the point of this. This is a cold, long, dangerous, dumb idea. I'd rather keep my limbs intact to ski tomorrow."

"Honey, I absolutely agree, go ahead on the bus," J. said. "I almost have to go along with the others, as one of the responsibles, and all that."

"I don't want to go on the bus! I don't want to go on the sled!" I cried, my panic intensifying as I saw I was now

doomed to this freakish adventure, clinging behind J., perhaps to be thrown into a chasm. For I also recognized that
I would have been ashamed of myself if I went on the bus
with the feeble elderly or inept young. Some deeply inter-
nalized sense of competition, or sport, or shame was prompt-
ing me, some invisible pressure of the group controlling me.
I was going to go against my will on this sled ride, J. too.
How could he go back on the bus if the other men slid down?
How was Dr. Prangithornbupu so blithely free from these
imperatives? We were going to do something perilous and
stupid because others were doing it. I shivered. I was already
cold, the night was icy, and I shivered too from fear and
compulsion. Why had I not inherited some of the intrepid
genes of my woman cousin who drove the Indy 500?

The organizers had now begun to notice, it seemed for the
first time, that many of their guests were underdressed, in
dinner shoes, gloveless, with no idea of how to direct a sled,
let alone in the dark on a long-distance track, and they began
to suggest that perhaps after all many would be more comfortable in the bus. At this, a certain perverse determination
required the guests to persist. All hope abandoned, their
wills stiffened with the courage of the desperate. Many people
were, I knew, attracted to danger and to proving themselves,
and even the most ordinary journey gives the traveler the
satisfying sense of dangers overcome and outlasted. It is one
of the charms of travel that mere cultural differences can
present themselves as dangers in order to provide this grat-
ifying sense of having survived them—I have survived, the
traveler can say: strange food, for example. I thought of eating
bats in Canton. All Chinese public toilets. Indian trains.
Swiss midnight downhill toboggan runs. I have survived,
therefore I will survive. Perhaps this was the whole point of

travel. But, even as this idea came to me, it came with the conviction that I didn't need to prove myself doing this. "Of course we're going to do it; besides, we paid for it," I heard someone remark in English.

"Honest, J., this isn't funny, people are going to get hurt," I said, hoping it would all be called off.

"That's why I need to go." I could see that he was angry. J. was brave but never foolhardy. "D., please go down on the bus."

"Deenee, eet weel be fun!" cried Huguette Cosset. "Come weeth me. I have done this toboggan, no, not here, but many times and I know well how to do it. You will sit behind me and be the brakes."

I had forgotten the insouciant attitude of the French toward danger. To go or not to go, and with J. or with Huguette? I eyed the tiny sled. J., large and long legged, would fill up his sled all by himself. I envisioned myself, ass dragging, bouncing off my pillory and over the cliff. Would J. mind, feel wounded, insulted, if I chose to go with Huguette? Did Huguette really want me? My ambivalence, already painful, now increased. Was Huguette really experienced, or was she—like other French people I had met—simply indifferent to danger and mad for sporty fun, or compelled by some cultural imperative of which Americans were unaware to feel that mentioning danger and seeming scared were to be scorned? I thought of another time I had been scared like this, skiing *hors piste* in France, in the spring, when the whole snowfield above us could be heard to groan with its need to break loose and slide down on us, and my French companions had laughed. It had seemed to me that their laughter was enough to bring the whole thing down with the vibrations of their merriment. As they led us deeper and deeper into the steep valley, I had wondered whether I was just a cowardly, stiff American or they were mad. But then, like now, I had been unwilling to go back, and fear had made me twist my knee, so that I greatly increased my chances of not being able to outski the expected avalanche. To my horror, I now noticed that Dr. Kora had pulled down a sled and was gazing intently at it with the beatified, dreamy expression of the Japanese kamikaze pilots depicted in American World War II movies. He was buttoning up his purple and white ski parka in a purposeful way, clearly intending to make the run. I worried; there was something fragile about little Dr. Kora, though I reassured myself that in Japan they had snow, that Dr. Kora skied well, and that he was probably less likely than tall J. to break his neck. Now Dr. Kora was smiling at Penny Deckhorne, and waving with bravado and laughing. The Deckhornes were taking separate sleds. The younger American doctors, professional as astronauts, were making short practice runs on a gentle hill to the left. The collective mind was now focused on survival.

The first to start out were gleeful, experienced Swiss, who whooped and called as they pushed off, their cries becoming fainter with chilling rapidity, which, according to Huguette, meant the track was fast. A perception of danger seemed to animate the Western Europeans generally into a special sort of gaiety; perhaps it was all those wars. I had often noticed the British attitude. When it came to the British, even the automobile seemed to inspire them, as if driving were a sport. I thought of those mad little cars with straps around the hoods. I wished now that I could bring myself to say to Huguette, "Perhaps J. would like me to go with him," though that was manifestly untrue.

I did not really expect to die—I did and I didn't. It was more the discomfort and possible broken bones that I minded.

Probably this was really less dangerous than skiing, which I do with reckless happiness. I drew breath and settled myself on the sled behind Huguette. I snuggled up as close as I could, but even so could feel that my bottom was quite near the back edge of the wooden seat.

"Get set. When I call to you, drag your feet, you are the brakes," Huguette reminded me.

"I'm ready," I said. As soon as I had wrapped my arms around Huguette, I was sorry not to be going with J. I could see him behind us, with his sled under his arm. J. could be reckless. I felt a stab of protective concern. Men felt obliged to be reckless, while women were safe. On this principle I had chosen to ride with Huguette. Yet I knew there was a flaw—the inbred recklessness of French people. The innate prudence of Americans ought to have directed me to choose differently. Did my defection mean I did not actually trust J.? When faced with a choice I had chosen life over loyalty, had preferred to take my chances on survival with Huguette rather than go down to disaster with J. But if we were to crash in a gully, wouldn't I have been better off with doctor J.? I despised myself for this selfish attitude of *sauve-qui-peut*. I was ashamed of the thoughts that flashed through my mind with a rush, like all the frames of a film superimposed on one another, producing a deep, jumbled shadow forest of images of destruction—all of them were of the impending snowy, icy, dark destruction that awaited us—if not myself, then J., or some elderly doctor gamely boarding his sled, or perhaps all of us, dashed like lemmings into the bottom of an icy crevasse.

Mind on death, I had not been prepared for the abruptness with which we went from a standing start to reckless speed, the icy night air filling my ears and lifting my hair, and billowing my coat with the wind that rushed down my neck.

Our runners made the noise of an underground stream, or of someone walking on an icy pond, dangerously crunching and cutting the ice. We were in utter darkness, careening through blackest space, with the saving mound of snow to the downhill side broken in places—perhaps places where others had crashed through it into the mountain chasms. "Brake, brake," Huguette called. Minutes of icy, rushing misery passed as we careered downward, my heels digging in as fiercely as I could make them, and seeming not to impede our speed.

It happened as my foreknowledge told me it would. With a lurch of the sled, a sharp banking of its angle, my arms loosened dreamlike from around Huguette, and I slipped from off the back, or the sled slipped from under me, so that in an instant I felt myself hit the rutted ice, and then bounce toward the mound of soft snow at the edge of the track. This gave way under me, and I tumbled, flailing, down a steep slope, the ice and rocks skinning the backs of my legs and the palms of my hands, and landed headfirst against the bare branches of a small tree ten feet below the embankment. I felt the crack of my forehead on the trunk.

In a minute I could tell that I was all right, though I thought I had hit my head quite badly. It all happened so fast that Huguette could not have realized I was gone, and could not anyway have stopped. Now I thought I heard her faint call. Only seconds had passed, but in the dream-sequence way that peril has of extending a moment, I already felt all the hazards of my situation, bruised, cold, and lost.

But I was not hurt, I soon decided, except for the sting of my palms. Snow had crowded into my boots and inside my underpants as I slid and now melted icily against my skin. Tears of chagrin filled my eyes at my own stupidity to have done this. Now I would have to wander down the track in the freezing dark, hoping to avoid being run down by others on their sleds, could maybe be picked up by someone coming with prudent slowness, digging his heels into the ice. I tried to find a handhold of shrubbery to help me scramble up the bank again. I should be glad, I knew, not to have fallen farther into the ravine.

It seemed for hours that I lurched and slipped on foot down the infinitely long mountain, shame and chagrin making me hide my face in my coat as people came by on their sleds. Snow trickled into my shoes, and my feet had begun to feel dangerously solid, as if they had frozen. It seemed to me the longest and most disagreeable experience of my life. Once, in Iran, I had been in peril of my life and been afraid, but those events had had a kind of interest, a stimulating effect. Now I understood why people lost in snowstorms simply stopped and froze in their tracks. The cold bores them, life comes to bore them as they stumble along, oppressed by the ennui of cold. If I stopped, I supposed, someone would find me, they would miss me at the bottom, Huguette would remark my absence. Yet I stumbled along. It must have been more than an hour, was perhaps hours before I saw the lights of a bus pulled into a clearing below me and heard the babble of languages that was probably my group.

J., surprisingly, was frightened. I saw the angry pinch of his nostrils, knew what his rough grasp of my arm meant. "You're freezing," he said, and, seeing my scratched forehead, "Did you hit your head?"

"No. Maybe," I said. "It hurts." I realized that my head hurt.

"Did you lose consciousness?"

"No. No, I'm fine."

J. peered at me. "How can I tell if it's concussion or hypothermia?" he snapped. "Go get in the bus."

Others were not accounted for—two Swiss men, news that the rest of the party received with a certain satisfaction. But Dr. Kora had not appeared either. Search parties began to climb upward along the toboggan run. It was another two hours before everyone was found, the Swiss doctor with a head injury that was possibly serious. Dr. Kora refused medical attention and did not thank the others for finding him. I had heard many stories like that, of lives saved, and the saved not thanking their saviors. I had heard it too often not to think there must be an inner reason people cannot thank others for their lives. Fearing to be bound to the saviors, perhaps, as the Chinese believe, or else moved beyond expression, unable to speak. That was my mood too, silent, going back to the hotel on the bus, in the Swiss night.

The Heart of Pakistan

The patient was dying, had been in a coma for some days now, and the situation was critical, for, if ever someone must be saved, this person must. Jimmy Carter himself was calling the illustrious heart transplant man at Baylor, to beg him to come. Could J. come tonight, if he could get a night plane to London, tomorrow at the latest, no expense spared—expense the very least of the worries—take the Concorde. "But I couldn't possibly," J. said. "Tomorrow I have—who is this person anyway?"

"I can't say on the phone," Randy Deckhorne said, in a James Bond tone. "You'll know when you get here."

The rest of us could hear J. on the phone in the other room. When he came back, he wore a pinkened look of amusement or excitement I recognized. "Randy Deckhorne asking me to fly to London tomorrow on the Concorde to see a Very Important Person whose name could not be mentioned."

As it happened, we were having English people to dinner—Lady Violet Denham and her husband, Carl, the thoracic surgeon, and an English journalist we knew, David Idem. In the manner of expatriates, the English perked up with nostalgic curiosity at the idea of who the VIP could be. Even for Dave, who had lived in the United States a long time, what happened in England had more reality and importance than what happened here.

"Couldn't you get any clue? Princess Margaret, I would think," Dave ventured.

"He just said he'd rather not say. But no expense spared and name your own fee."

"What fun, I wish I were going to London tomorrow," Lady Violet said.

"Can you get on the Concorde at such short notice?"

"But I'm not *going*!" said J., amazed they would think him somebody at the beck of unnamed royals, to be persuaded for a fee to leave his own important work. Since J. does not have a private practice, he is more or less immune to the promise of money, and was deplorably—so I felt—free from low curiosity about the identity of the famous sick person.

"You're bloody crazy," Carl Denham said. "A couple of days in London, why not? Maybe they'd pay for D. too." This involved my emotions directly, for I would much prefer a weekend in London to one in San Francisco, as who would not?

"A hoot," Violet agreed. "Though the Concorde is detestable."

"Randy said that Jimmy Carter is trying to persuade Calvin Markham, the heart man at Baylor. They're assembling an international team," J. said. I could see that, despite his refusal, he was glad to have been asked.

"You could see the big Constable show at the Royal Academy," Violet said. "I wish it was me going. And I haven't done me Marks and Spencer run yet this year."

"Think about it, J.," I pleaded. "At least ask them if you could bring me."

We could see the idea was gaining on him. He went to

call Randy Deckhorne again, and in the end was persuaded. While the rest of us ate our dessert, and after J. had served the cognac, he went to call British Airways.

It was reassuring, exciting even, to find someone waiting for us at Heathrow, at the exit to customs, a liveried man holding a sign for J. "I'm Ron," he said. "I'll take you to the hotel, sir, the lady can get settled, but then I'll be driving you directly to the hospital." His car was a red Mercedes stretch, which struck us as not being what we had expected, a little too flashy, portending other surprises, even disappointments. Arabs, perhaps. Then we were briefly disappointed that the hotel was the Hilton; like the red limousine, this did not predict English royals, though it didn't suggest Arabs necessarily. The suite was luxurious, with flowers and fruit awaiting us, but no champagne, which did suggest Arabs. J. splashed water on his face and went back downstairs, where Ron was smartly waiting, the car poised on the forecourt, right outside the doors. Arabs positively, I thought— someone rich enough to be allowed to drop spots of oil on the Hilton forecourt.

In the car, Ron dialed a number on his car phone and whispered, though J. could hear him, "I'm bringing Dr. M. over right now." They approached Queen's Hospital Cromwell. J. recognized it, though it had been built long after his fellowship at Hammersmith—a well-equipped private hospital where Harley Street physicians and important professors and consultants could confidently avert for their paying patients the democratic privations of the National Health Service hospitals.

A dark man in a white coat was waiting inside the revolving doors to the lobby. He stepped out and opened the car door for J. "Hello, Doctor, I am Dr. Marsa. I will take you right up to see the patient. The other physicians are assembling at this moment, and you can join them when you have completed your examination."

The patient, by the look of his grizzled gray hair and dark skin, was a man of some Middle Eastern nationality, in his late fifties or early sixties. Sixty-two, Dr. Marsa said. The man was comatose and on a respirator, arrayed with the conventional numbers of tubes and monitors. In the room two nurses sat, one on each side of the bed, and, despite the monitors, one kept her fingers on the man's wrist. On either side of the door stood men in business suits, with the wary expressions of bodyguards.

J. performed an examination while Dr. Marsa told him the history. The man was a banker, Dr. Marsa said. J. knew that I would be disappointed to hear that.

"He is head of a bank, one of the most important banks in the world, and especially important when it comes to loans for developing countries, and for the Middle East. This is why your former President Carter has called upon Dr. Markham at Baylor, and yourself, and others," he said. "Many important figures are concerned about our patient, concerned that he rise from this condition and return to himself. The fact is, he is not a man to rely on others, and some of the most important details of his international doings, these complicated details, are in his head only. Only he knows what he knows. And of course there is the anguish of his family and friends, the purely humanitarian concerns for this good man.

"He had a heart attack four weeks ago in Karachi. He was hospitalized there, and at first seemed to do well. Then his condition began to worsen, he had several episodes of cardiac arrest during which he became comatose, and it is as you see. Finally it was decided that we in Pakistan could do no more, and he was brought here. The king of Saudi Arabia sent his seven-forty-seven to bring him here."

J. recognized that the names of kings and presidents were being wielded to impress him, yet he was impressed. There was nothing about the man to suggest his extraordinary status. He could have been any face in a crowd of demonstrators in a newsreel from Baghdad, or a member of some cadre of Middle Eastern secret police, his square face and worn fingers peasantlike, his body paunchy.

J. was accustomed to the phenomenon by which a comatose person on these machines is diminished, deprived of selfhood, reduced to the common denominator of his clay. Only by being told could J. imagine him powerful, in control, brain packed with secrets, and it was only in the symbols of his power—the limousines, the Concorde, these measures of the value set upon him by others—that his power could be understood. To all of this he must himself be indifferent. Probably, J. judged, he wouldn't survive this crisis. He asked for the X rays, read the results of the lab work, came to a conclusion in a very few minutes. The case was even rather obvious. He followed Dr. Marsa, who said, "I'll take you downstairs now, sir, to join the others."

An even more dramatic measure than the Concorde of the patient's influence and wealth was the assemblage of famous physicians seated in the conference room, around a mahogany table appointed in the manner of a comfortable English gentlemen's club, a litter of coffee cups and papers arrayed before them. A dozen doctors, some of whom J. knew— Randy Deckhorne, of course, and Robert Brian, the neurologist from Boston; and the famed cardiac surgeon Calvin Markham; a third, from St. Louis University, J. had heard of; and the British renal man, Tomkins, whom J. had known from their Hammersmith days. The others were introduced.

Several had Pakistani names—these were evidently the team from Karachi who had been in on his case from the first. The Americans, in from great distances, were lightly unshaven and serious. The English doctors wore elegant pinstripes, custom tailored, the jackets slightly flared, side vented, not American-looking suits. Two nations, separated by tailoring and those ties symbolizing their pasts of privilege and privation in some public school. J., Brian, and Markham wore similar tweed jackets, and Rockports. The Pakistani doctors wore English suits. J. observed that the English doctors practiced an elaborate courtesy with the Pakistani doctors that seemed to him a little patronizing.

One of the Pakistani doctors, Dr. Pachiar, explained that the discussion had just begun. They were reviewing, organ by organ, the condition and prospects of the patient; each doctor would recommend treatment, a consensus would be arrived at. "We have come to the kidney," he said. "Dr. Tomkins, please continue, and then, Dr. M., we will hear from you."

"I should say at once," said J. when his turn came, "that I think, if he is to survive at all, he will need a new heart."

"Yes," said Dr. Pachiar, "it is the conclusion to which we are all coming. In fact we might proceed from here with that as our hypothesis. We will discuss the pros and cons of heart transplantation. I beg you, take issue with this, raise the negatives." But, as the discussion proceeded, there did not seem to be any negatives, or rather, any alternatives, and indeed some questioned whether the patient could be kept alive while he waited in turn for a heart. "He," they called him, religiously. The actual name, Abedi, mentioned once, had not meant anything to J.

"What about the family? Will they consent?" J. asked at one point, thinking there might perhaps be a religious or cultural difficulty. He was remembering a case he had had involving an Indian youth who had been mugged in the United States—had been murdered—and was brain dead though kept alive on a respirator. The family when asked about donating his strong heart and kidneys had said they could not agree because they were Hindu, and Hindus did not permit the bodies of their dead to be cut into and desecrated. J. could not remember if Pakistanis were ever Hindus, or what the Muslim view was. The rules of these religions were something he absolutely could never keep straight.

He was struck by how, at the mention of the family, the conversation faltered a little. J. had found that obtaining consent was often the trickiest part of any procedure—explaining carefully, considering the feelings of the people who must give consent, presenting the issues. The English and Pakistani doctors looked surprised that J. should mention consent, as if they had never thought of it.

"Has he a family? A wife?" J. went on.

"Yes, of course. There is a wife. She is here. But I do not think that is really an issue we need consider," said Dr. Pachiar. "Perhaps you could talk to her?"

This was his punishment, J. saw, for bringing up an inconvenient matter. He pictured the possible wife—a village wife, old, stout, commanding, wearing one of those tunic-trouser suits; or an English airline stewardess, a likelier possibility; or perhaps there were several wives. He also could not remember, or perhaps had never known, the domestic arrangements in Pakistan regarding plural wives.

The discussion was in fact informative—a dozen great specialists showing off the minutiae and sophistication of their knowledge, and the medical details were interesting. Heart transplantation lay outside J.'s everyday preoccupations. It was excitingly dramatic, impressively complex. He liked to have input from time to time about these advanced surgical procedures far from his own specialty. He in his turn discussed the condition of the lungs and the immune situation.

Now that it had been decided what to do with the corporeal Mr. Abedi, a single question remained unanswered: to what extent his brain had been damaged by oxygen deprivation associated with the episodes of heart stoppage. To what extent could he recover, even if his heart were new? He might recover physiologically and yet be mentally a vegetable. It would not be possible for him to regain consciousness until the circulation was restored to his brain; yet that could not happen without a new heart. In the meantime, it was decided to support his own damaged heart and to raise his blood pressure with a balloon-assisted pump. This would require an operation, which would be scheduled for the next morning.

"We will just have to await results," the principal Pakistani doctor summed up, an anxious preoccupation settling over his features as he thought of what lay ahead. "We would like to meet in the morning, if you please. I know, Dr. Markham is flying back this afternoon, but if the rest of us could meet. . . . I thank each of you gentlemen for the inconvenience to which you have submitted, and for your care in coming here."

"Actually, the wife has no rights in Pakistan," Randy Deckhorne told J. as they left the room. "Interesting, no? If our patient dies, as is jolly likely, it's all up with her. She'll have nothing. So I wonder what she'll say? She might prefer a living vegetable, at least she'd still be a wife. Not that it matters, they'll operate anyhow. In Pakistan, the wives are considered to be property, like the Rolls-Royces. I learned all this when Penny did her anthropology course."

"All the same, she ought to be asked." It shocked J. to hear Randy adopt the callous tone you would not have expected from a pillar of Harley Street, trained to be responsive to the human side of medicine and to the feelings of wives.

Randy laughed and clapped J. on the shoulder. "I remember reading about Rajiv Gandhi, how when the prime ministers of the assembled nations have something unpleasant to take up with Mrs. Thatcher, they send Rajiv because they consider him the best looking and hence the most likely to get round her." At this non sequitur J.'s puzzlement must have shown in his face. "That's why you get the job of talking to Mrs. Abedi." Randy laughed.

Mrs. Abedi and her daughter were waiting for J. in the sitting room of what appeared to be a sumptuous hotel suite in the rear wing of the hospital. She was graciously arrayed on a sofa when a servant showed him in but jumped up with great alacrity to greet him. A beautiful, dark-eyed woman in her thirties and a pudgy teenager of a muddy, darker complexion behind her. Both were dressed in expensive-looking Western clothes, as far as J.'s judgment of these things went.

Mrs. Abedi asked if J. would like tea, and directed a servant to bring some. He would have liked a beer, but it seemed unsuited to the occasion. After some preliminaries, he explained the grave course the medical team had decided on, outlined the risks, asked for her views. Her questions were intelligent, her tendency optimistic.

"He must come back—and so I am sure he will." She smiled. "I know you do wonderful things now."

"This operation is much, much more successful than even two years ago. The progress has been enormous. But it is still an operation with a very high risk."

"If he has the heart of another—this is something I am wondering—will he still be himself, or will he be someone else?"

"That's hard to say," J. admitted, thinking she spoke of personality changes, brain damage. "He will be on a heart-lung machine that will oxygenate his brain. The danger is that he has sustained brain damage already."

"We speak of the heart as being the seat of the most intimate self," she said, "but of course it isn't, that is the brain."

"Yes," J. agreed.

"I know we must do everything, everything to help him," she said. "Only I hope it will not be terrible—for *him*, you know, I mean." Suddenly she turned to her daughter and spoke to her in their language—would it be Urdu?—and the girl left the room. When she turned again to J., Mrs. Abedi's eyes were filled with tears.

How vulnerable she was, J. thought, and not only because of her position. He could see that her heart was in anguish, and that her affection for her husband was real. "The waiting," he said. "To begin with, it can be quite some time before a heart is found. His case is urgent, so he'll be given a priority, obviously, over someone who could safely wait longer, who is in a less grave condition. Even so, he has a rare blood type, which will pose another problem."

"Does it ever happen that a heart is not found in time?"

"Yes, often, I'm sorry to say. And even if a heart is found, you have to remember the risks, and that the failures far outnumber the successful outcomes. This is surgery of the most desperate kind."

"Oh"—she sighed—"I cannot get that ever out of my mind."

J. left the hospital with a certain sense of anticlimax. To have flown thousands of miles for fifteen minutes with a man in a coma and twelve other doctors, to attend a discussion in which his own views were by no means the most germane, seemed not the best employment of his time, was a little frivolous, in fact. He thought of the desperately ill patients he had left at home. Rather than because anyone had need of his views, this convocation of doctors seemed almost to have been arranged for the sake of protocol or decorum, so that someone somewhere would be able to say that everything, everything had been done.

But he was happy to have been able to reassure the lovely wife, she who would so soon be ownerless chattel. He hoped she had salted something away, though she did not seem like the sort of calculating woman who would have; quite the opposite, she seemed high-minded and intelligent. Her face stayed in his mind as Ron drove him back to the Hilton. She had an oval face, the shape of a cameo, the hair parted in the middle, huge brown eyes, like the soulful eyes of a figure on a Grecian tomb.

"I have taken Madam to the National Gallery, and am to pick her up at six," Ron said, talking of me.

"Tell her I'll be in the bar," J. said, springing out of the car before Ron could get out and come around to open the door.

It was a fine thing to have an unexpected day in London, and a car to drive me. I stuffed my parcels on the empty chair next to J. in the bar and sat in another, surrounded by green sacks from Marks & Spencer and Laura Ashley, purple Liberty parcels—all the London errands I could think of for our family and some errands for Violet Denham. J. told me about his meeting, the patient, the beautiful, mournful Mrs. Abedi, and the fate that awaited her after the probable death of her husband—to be a piece of property sent back to Pakistan with nothing, while officials of the bank and a bevy of doctors divided up her fortune. I felt myself a trifle irritated by his excessive solicitude.

"Nonsense, J., she could be a professor at London University, you don't know anything about her. Maybe she comes from a rich family in Pakistan, probably does, they all marry each other. Maybe they had a prenuptial agreement sparing her from being chattel. Maybe her dowry will be returned to her. What would Randy Deckhorne know about it?" I could hear that my voice had a slight edge to it, as if I were speaking of a rival. "Anyway, aren't you going to save him?"

"Heart transplants are hardly an everyday, reliable sort of operation."

"How long are we staying then?" I asked. "This is divine. The greatest thing is Ron, that is, having a driver. He's a cat fancier. I had no idea it would make such a difference having a driver. I went to both the Tate and the National Gallery."

"Well, I'm going to shower," said J., suddenly looking tired and jet-lagged. Randy Deckhorne had invited us to a dinner at the Royal Society of Medicine. "He's Sir Randy now, he's been knighted somewhere along the way," J. said. "Do you have a flowered dress?"

"Flowered dress? No. Why?"

"I don't know, I've just always noticed that the English ladies all wear flowered dresses. Haven't you ever noticed that?"

I hadn't, but at the dinner I saw that it was true—large, blonde women all in flowered silks, with pearls, and the imposing, red-faced men. I liked the English, with their hooting, stammering voices, their toasts, their Stilton and port, their light morals. I admired how they said grace in Latin and leapt to their feet when someone said, "To the queen!" They are supposed to be like us, or we like them, but I find them exotic. I think the French are much more like us than the English are, despite the language, if only because we both had revolutions, and seem less concerned about class and accents.

As the blood-poisoning effect of air travel set in, we drooped through the after-dinner speeches; then, with the unpredictable action of jet-deranged hormones, we came wide awake as Ron drove us back to the hotel and sat up watching the midnight television news. At some celebration during the day, a choir had sung "Vivat, Vivat, Regina Elizabetha," the replay now ringing out on the cable network. "Remembering that her family goes back to Owen Glendower and Robert the Bruce, George Washington and Robert E. Lee," said the commentator. It seemed a funny thing to tell a British audience.

J. remarked how England had changed since the days of his fellowship at Hammersmith Hospital. I thought over the day, the dignified brown faces of people on the streets of London, their humming, strange, rapid typewriter–sounding English, if indeed they were speaking English. As an American you were obliged to think London had changed for the better by becoming pluralistic, filled with rich smells of curry and *bolito misto*, but you did have to wonder if it seemed better to the English.

We woke, of course, at four in the morning, divided a sleeping pill between us, and went back to sleep until seven. We had breakfast in the room, then J. went down. Ron, who gave the impression of living only for us, was waiting to take him to the hospital. Did each of the other doctors have a separate Ron? As they drove, J. calculated the plane fares alone for the half-dozen American specialists, and the probable fee of Calvin Markham, who was said to earn twenty thousand for a single operation, of which he could have done six or seven in the time he had been here. Hotel bills, fees, and, for each, a Ron in a limousine. From his mirrored car window he looked out with new fellowship at the pink, freshly barbered English faces looking out of Rollses and Mercedeses as they drew adjacent in the circle of Marble Arch traffic.

At the door of Abedi's room, the bodyguards did not let him go in.

"I'm one of his doctors," J. said.

"The patient is not here."

"Not here?" Dead? J. was startled, though many explanations occurred to him—he could be downstairs for a CAT scan or an MRI. "Where is he?"

"He's in the operating theater." Probably they were implanting the balloon counterpulsation pump. "They are performing the transplantation," the man continued.

J. was thunderstruck. He stood, with a stupefied expression, unable to believe that a decision made fourteen hours before could already have been implemented. How could they have found a heart, let alone a B-positive heart, in this short time? He had visions of armed men in dark alleys waylaying late-night revelers. And how could they have overridden all the procedures and protocols by which people waited in turn for hearts?

At this, a sort of fury boiled up in J., a feeling of having been duped into displacing himself to assist in rubber-stamping a decision that must have been well under way before he and the others flew in. Angrily, he went down the hall to the nurses' station, had Randy Deckhorne paged, and waited for him in the admitting lobby.

"I guess we'll be off," J. said, his fury clear in his voice. "There isn't really much I can do at this point. How is the operation going?"

"Fantastically kind of you to come, J., I so much appreciate it, and the Abedis do, obviously. Do stay another day or two, of course, now that you're here, you and D., and keep Ron if you like. And the hotel, everything."

"Thanks, but I have to get back," said J., still tight-lipped, and not planning to tell me about this offer. "Randy—how did you get a heart in twelve hours?"

Here it seemed to J. that a flicker of evasive calculation preceded Randy's reassuring smile. "Oh, we can almost always get hearts in an emergency. The communication—it's all computerized now, you send out an alert. The fact is, a lot of hearts go to waste for lack of recipients, isn't it the same in the States?"

"Awfully good luck finding a B-positive one."

"I know," Randy said, their eyes meeting for a fraction of a second, during which J. could read in Randy's eyes, he almost thought, something of his own surprise. And, it now seemed to J., there was in Randy's voice a note of embarrassment, or perhaps it was J.'s own emotion in Randy's behalf, or his own, that they would bend the rules for a sheik with a jet, that England now had to do things England wouldn't have done before. But, nonsense, any man, rich or poor, could get health care in England, wasn't that a glory of the nation?

Even so, a poor man would not get a new heart in a day, no way. And in the United States a rich man wouldn't either, he would wait his turn. J. felt a small tickle of satisfaction at that, and of pity for them all, though less for himself, of course, because he had come for friendship, not money. And presumably Jimmy Carter, making those phone calls, would say the same.

We had lunch at the Tate, with our old friends Hilary and Philip, in the beautiful dining room under the Rex Whistler murals, drank an especially fine bottle of Bordeaux, charged to Mr. Abedi, and told the story of our two-day junket to London and the mysterious heart. We returned to the mystery of where the heart had come from. Philip fancifully proposed that the heart came from a secret tontine. "An organ tontine. You hire a hundred Pakis, you pay each of them a stipend, year in, year out, on the condition that should you need an organ, and should his number come up, it's his kidney, his liver that you get. Only some poor devil had to donate his heart. Or, in some alley in Leicester—that's where they all live—some Pakistani youth is jumped by thugs and left for dead. He is brought in by soi-disant bystanders. Then, by coincidence, the doctors hear that there's a call for a B-positive heart."

J. was chilled by this laughter, for this same fear, inarticulated, had plagued him, and perhaps Randy Deckhorne too. Yet such things could not be, and, certainly, one could not be, however inadvertently, a part of them. That was too horrible, and, after all, too unlikely, in an advanced country in the twentieth century. It was his own collusion against the grain, bought, after all, by the prospect of an amusing two days in London for me, that made him uneasy—evidence that people will act against their principles for money. He told himself, reminded himself, that he had done it for Randy Deckhorne, and, perhaps, for Jimmy Carter, and out of a sense of adventure and curiosity that was not exactly the same as cupidity. But he was uneasy.

We had arranged for tickets on the Concorde flight that took off at dinnertime, and left for Heathrow early enough to stop at Ron's house to meet his cat, fulfilling a promise I had made.

"Five minutes, just to meet her," Ron said. "It's just on the way. Madam and I have talked quite a bit about cats."

His place was a large ground-floor flat in Pimlico. A beautiful Persian cat met us at the door. "My wife's out, I guess. Anyway, this is Priscilla. The wife takes her to cat shows and the like. She does quite well. We plan to breed her."

His kitchen was fitted and new. The walls of the parlor were decorated with faience plates from the Algarve and Mexico. He brought out photos of Priscilla's kittenhood. J. could hardly bear all this, was desperate to get on the plane. At the airport he gave Ron a fifty-dollar bill, without any idea if it was too much or too little.

On the plane our sense of being on a lark gave in to fatigue, and I had the frightening thought that Mr. Abedi would die and his estate, tied up for all time in thickets of litigation, would be unable to pay for our airplane tickets, twelve thousand dollars we had charged on our American Express. J. was tired too, and an image of corruption bore upon him. He had gone to London for friendship, of course, but he had gone for the hell of it, too, and, he saw, he had gone because he had wanted to fly on the Concorde. This last real motivation seared him with its shallowness; he had been bought, was being bought, and for a price probably cheaper than the English charged at that. J. was not normally introspective, but, when he did inspect his own morality, he expected to find it excellent. Instead—here it was. He'd been bought for a trip on the Concorde. Later he admitted that it crossed his mind, as he ordered a gin martini, that it was actually my fault that we had done this, and that it was I who was shallow and frivolous.

After a few days he called Randy Deckhorne from his office for an update on the patient's condition. Mr. Abedi was alive but had never returned to himself, refused to speak to anyone, and no one knew if he could.

It was a month after this that I heard something on the news that startled us both, about the exposure of a giant money-laundering operation the Feds had been watching for years. Officers of the Bank of Credit and Commerce were arrested in Miami, Panama, London, and Luxembourg for handling Colombian drug profits, slipping them thither and yon, over their wires, in strange certificates of purchase and back-to-back loans. I got the newspaper, which didn't say much more, but showed photographs of people being led from banks, hands on heads. Their names were Hispanic or Pakistani. GIANT BUST BREAKS DRUG SCHEME. The BCCI was Mr. Abedi's bank. I called J. at the hospital.

"Mr. Abedi is a drug lord." I explained what I had heard.

"Jimmy Carter couldn't have known that" was J.'s first response. "Nor Mrs. Abedi."

After this, it seemed that J. somehow couldn't stop thinking about the Abedi case. He mentioned it often. I think it upset him to be a part of evil. To have been at the beck of evil. It stayed on his mind, the panoply of tailored English doctors with the pink faces, the suave Asians, Calvin Markham, himself, and the other Americans in their brown shoes. He had a picture of them sitting around the table, conducting that high-priced conversation, doctors piously concerned about human life, rich or poor. That the life should have been a drug lord's he hardly knew how to calculate into his own moral scheme. He remembered stories about Howard

Hughes's doctors, respectable Mormons, and about how Hughes had doctors on call, living in his place; he had never understood why a doctor would do that, and here he himself had done it, had consecrated a day—three days, really—to a drug lord. It filled him with shame, and an obscure anger at me that took some months to assuage.

Rolex

J. had gone to a meeting in Washington; I had begged off for once and was reveling in the quiet mornings at home, and the chance to work undisturbed on a novel I was writing. Then he telephoned to say he had forgotten to tell me that I would be getting a visit from someone named Yan Zhang, or Zhang Yan, who was coming to San Francisco, and could we put up this Yan Zhang for a couple of days? Yan was a young woman doctor we had met in Beijing—I would remember when I saw her. J. had had a letter from Dr. Lixing Wang in China about her, and then Yan Zhang herself had called him. She had been in the United States for several months, studying in Houston, and was planning a visit to San Francisco. She said she had something for me and wanted to deliver this item personally. J.'s voice expressed curiosity, but I could not guess what the item might be.

And naturally J. had proposed that she stay with us. I said of course. The reflex of traveling in foreign lands is that eventually people are likely to turn up in San Francisco. I more than J. bore the brunt of entertaining them, for no one imagined that a doctor would interrupt his work; I would try to make them as comfortable as possible, and drive them to see the Golden Gate Bridge, Muir Woods, and the Palace of the Legion of Honor. While receiving kindnesses in foreign lands, I always vowed to make myself endlessly hospitable in return. At home, however, our visitors never failed to come at a bad moment, testing this resolution. I tried to behave as graciously as possible, but was never without a sense of shame, knowing myself to feel inconvenienced. Of course I understood that J. and I were just as inconvenient for them.

On the appointed Saturday, the doorbell rang at seven-thirty in the morning. The children were eating their cereal, and I was idly reading the paper, and for a moment couldn't imagine who it could be. A young Chinese woman—small, newly permanented, wearing a maroon gabardine pantsuit that had certainly come from China, styleless, vaguely military, reminding of schoolteachers or certain orders of South American nuns. Her face was familiar—we had certainly met her in China. I thought maybe she had been the assistant of our host, Dr. Wang, the chief of the Department of Infectious Diseases in the hospital that J. was visiting. She had come to the many banquets and had once, if I remembered, taken me to some of the stores along the Wangfujing street. Now I smiled and welcomed her, but, though J. had told me, I could not remember the name until the woman said it.

"I'm Yan Zhang. Do you remember? Did you hear from Dr. Wang?" She held out a little manila envelope. "In it you will find your lost watch." She smiled, watching for my delighted reaction. Instead, I felt a moment of complete blankness. I did not believe I had lost a watch, could not remember one.

"Thank you so much," I said anyway. "It's so wonderful of you. Please come in." I laid the envelope on the table and helped Dr. Zhang with her small suitcase. "J. says you will be able to stay a day or two?"

"I can stay until Wednesday," said Dr. Zhang. "I am most

eager to see your city, for I have heard it is very lovely. I am studying in Houston."

"How nice," I said. I made her some tea and toast, and asked her for news of Dr. Wang, and of Dr. Lo-wan Liu, the doctor from Canton, and Dr. Tong-jing Ng, the one who had taken us to the acrobats and the Chinese opera. This was the extent of the names I could remember. I felt, as we talked, a wave of nostalgia for Beijing, where I had spent a happy month living in the old Beijing Hotel, a rambling assemblage of several hotels near Tiananmen Square, venerable home of all journalists and business travelers, and minor foreign diplomats waiting for quarters in the city.

I had spent an autumn month, doing a little writing in the mornings, then in the afternoons wandering the Beijing streets, dodging bicycles, a scarf tied over my hair, leading the life of an anonymous observer of the doings of the capital. I stood in line to gaze at the corpse of Mao Tse-tung. I admired the fanciful temples, the faded cinnabar color of the buildings, the pounded grassless paths to the pagodas, and the little alleys where people persevered in their old-fashioned lives, with their piles of cabbages and little braziers puffing away among ugly new apartments on every side. The air of the mornings was damp with the tons of fresh washing hung out from all the windows. In the dingy department stores I could spend hours weighing a purchase of silk undershirts or feather coats, or embroidery turned out by numberless women in the provinces.

At first I had minded the infantilizing and powerless state of being unable to speak or read in which I passed my days, gesturing with signs and feeling frightened when I lost my way. I learned the simplest Chinese characters, for exit, entrance, woman, and I learned to say a word that sounded to me like *neeehowma*, hello, but I felt like an imposter saying it, hardly able to believe that such an odd sound could denote anything at all, or as if words were meaningless unless you understood them in your heart.

At other times, here as in other places where I could not speak or understand, I enjoyed this exclusion from language. In Persia I had learned to count, to thank, to greet, to write my name in the beautiful undulating script; but I was defeated by Chinese before I started, by the characters like inscrutable decoration, and the long nasal vowels and singing tones. Since it was meaningless to me, as devoid of signification as music, the words were as pure, as restful and lovely.

During the month I lost my fear of the strangeness of a country where I couldn't read the signs; I philanthropically traded my hard currency for the local tattered yen and bought on the open market instead of in the Friendship Stores. It was the index of my adjustment that even Chinese art, which seemed so horrible in the beginning, began to look all right to me. At first I had been repelled by embroidered panda handkerchiefs and porcelain gnomes. Now, kimono dolls and rooms decorated in violent red and gold did not look peculiar to me. Dragons knitted onto pillow covers, and ponds filled with strange, cement-colored rocks—it all seemed lovely. I came to understand calligraphy. I visited a needlework school. A hundred women embroidered kittens in microscopic stitches on transparent silk and sandwiched them in round frames set on little pedestals, and these looked natural and nice to me, though I knew I would lose this delusion when I got back, and didn't make the mistake of buying any panda handkerchiefs or kittens for my friends. For them I bought lacquer boxes and lapis necklaces. But what happened to the elegant aesthetic of Sung, of Tang? This puzzle remains intriguing to me. And I learned to eat whatever was served, without inquiring, depriving our hosts of the pleasure they seemed to feel in shocking Westerners with the revelation that they have just eaten bat or snake. Anyway, it seemed to me, once cut up in little pieces, all things, whether badger or toad, tasted remarkably alike.

In the evenings, J. and I would drink in the lobby bar in the hotel, where all the other foreigners did too. There you met people from countries you wouldn't expect—an oil salesman from Iran, suave in Western tailoring, who had defended the war with Iraq; and a violent German girl who denounced America's involvement in Vietnam with such persistence, though she surely had not been born then, that J. had been finally goaded into asking if she had heard of Nazis. Most of the foreigners were nice—jolly Dutch backpackers, people staying elsewhere in the city in youth hostels who came in here for the camaraderie of European voices. Westerners could walk in and out of the Beijing Hotel with impunity, and I had not at first realized that a Chinese person could not just come in and order a drink, the guards outside would prevent it.

All Chinese did not look alike to me, each one looked different. This happened all at once, in a moment, as with one of those puzzles with hidden shapes you cannot see until suddenly you see them and then cannot not see. I found the Chinese merry and stoic, and I concealed the number of my purchases from them, so that my extravagances would not offend. They were so poor, and wore their work clothes to dinners. Professor Wang, the greatest professor of medicine in all of China, lived in two rooms, and his dining table was made from boards set atop the television set. A bed was pushed into the corner. The Wangs had four books only — one a photo album, with cuttings of Western reviews of a novel written by Mrs. Wang's grandmother in the thirties.

They had saved it by hiding it during the Cultural Revolution, when it could have been dangerous having a grandmother who wrote books.

While Dr. Zhang drank her tea, I opened the manila envelope containing the watch. With surprise I realized that it was my Rolex. Not a real Rolex of course, a fake one I had accidentally left behind in the Beijing Hotel; it hadn't even been worth writing to ask about it. I had hoped the porter or the maid had found it, and now, instead, here it was, more than a year later, returned to me still ticking, set on Chinese time. I thanked Yan Zhang over and over, my amazement passing, I hoped, for happiness to have my valuable treasure back again. Indeed, I *was* amazed, and tried to imagine the chain of events that could have brought it back to me. "How on earth did you find it? What a lot of trouble you've been to. How careless of me to have left it," I exclaimed.

Of course I had forgotten about it. I had bought it in Singapore, shopping with Huguette Cosset, who like all Frenchwomen had a carnet of good addresses collected from other Frenchwomen—where to get the good jewelry, and the name of the good tailor, the handmade shoes, the Mont-Blancs, and the watches. The best copy watches, almost indistinguishable from the *vrai*, guaranteed to work a year or two, made wonderful presents, everyone loved them. You could have Gucci, or Cartier, Rolex, whatever, for ten dollars. I hadn't planned to buy one, if only because they were illegal and you had to smuggle them into the United States—I had heard of people having them confiscated. The wives of customs officials wore them, I supposed.

Huguette and I had found the shopping mall with great difficulty. Singapore, which I had imagined as a steamy, palm-lined, vine-covered tropic, with louvered jalousies, verandas, planter's punches and sloe gin, had instead been entirely torn down, if it had ever existed outside of Maugham stories and old movies, and been replaced by shopping malls and giant hotels. One mall was much like another; the hotels outdid one another in vastness, in the chilly, tomblike marble vaulting of their opulent lobbies, in the grandeur and authenticity of the European antiques carted across the Pacific to furnish the lobbies, and in the whimsy of their theme restaurants. J. and I clung to Raffles, the seedy survivor of more colorful days, but it looked like Raffles's time was about up too. Digging machines stood by in the garden, and there was no net on the tennis court.

In search of the New Horizon Shopping Center, Huguette and I wandered the boulevards, though it was quite obvious that you weren't meant to wander, were meant to have a car, or go in a taxi. It could have been Los Angeles. "Singapore is the oogliest place I ever was," said Huguette. "I am so glad we went to Thailand first, or, otherwise, this would be my sole idea of *l'Asie*, what a pity." We laughed when at last we found the New Horizon Shopping Center, and, even more miraculously, the proper shop, from among the hundreds of little shops on endless floors, "Mr. Woon"—she had written it down. Inside it was even funnier because there were French people Huguette knew from Paris! Gilles and Marie-Anne Donon! And the Donons had seen Frederic Barsac coming out as they came in. I watched irritation or mystification suffuse the features of the shopkeeper, Madame Woon, if it was she, at the French chatter she could not understand. Perhaps.

The French exchanged several anecdotes of local shopping, then, "*Au travail*," cried Huguette, returning to the business at hand. "May I see the watches?"

"*Regardez les superbes Cartiers,*" cried Madame Donon, spreading out her Cartiers for Huguette to see. "*Ils ont toutes les bonnes marques françaises.*"

In the end, I had been drawn in too. What better ten-dollar present could you take someone? The watches were perfect, absolutely indistinguishable from real. We turned them over and over, admiring them. It was hard to choose—Patek Philippe, Mercier and Baum, Gucci, Tiffany—in the end I bought two men's Cartiers for joke Christmas presents, a Rolex for myself, and a Gucci for my friend B. A few times, during the afternoon, I had taken my Rolex out of my purse and looked closely at it. How did I know it was not really real? It appeared to have tiny diamonds and little dots of luminescent paint to mark each number. ROLEX OYSTER PERPETUAL DATEJUST, it said, and in letters almost too tiny to read I had later with a magnifying glass read SUPERLATIVE CHRONOMETER OFFICIALLY CERTIFIED. There was a little window at three o'clock, through which you read the date. Perhaps this was the real Rolex, put into the batch by mistake? I had laughed at myself for even thinking the thought, but I had thought it. In fact I had a kind of interest in watches. I was once in Hong Kong for three weeks, and after the third day there is little else to do but marvel at the profusion of watches, the little glittering diamanté ones, and big gold ones, onyx, steel, silver, water-resistant, waterproof, quartz, jeweled, bracelet, pendant, men's, women's, sport, dress, alarm . . .

At the dinner that evening, all the French women were wearing attractive, expensive-looking watches, their husbands too; all wrists were girded with imposing Rolexes and Tissots, and there was much merriment and comparing. J. had been disapproving, saying, "Isn't it a little—well—why would you want to pretend you had a Rolex?" very priggishly.

"Why would you even want a Rolex?" But he softened his attitude a little when he saw that it was some kind of French joke I had entered into.

While Huguette and I shopped, J.'s meeting, the quarterly meeting of the International Infectious Diseases Council, adjourned its deliberations for the afternoon at the request of the Thai, Dr. Sungsam Prangithornbupu. Although the council did not usually do fieldwork, Dr. Prangithornbupu urged them to look at first hand into some of the conditions that might be contributing to the inexplicable deaths of young men from Thailand who had come to work in Singapore only to die mysteriously in their sleep. There were hundreds of these deaths now, young men who cried out in their sleep; and the other men in the bare bunkhouses heard them and rushed to find them dead. Coming back to the hotel before dinner, J. had told me about the shacks of tin and straw, with water from the pump and a poor rice diet cooked on open fires in the mud streets behind the modern shopping centers, invisible.

"These boys do not live as well as my dogs in Thailand," Dr. Prangithornbupu had angrily said.

The local public health man, Lee, had brought a boy named Sridor to tell them about his friend Potha. Sridor, they could see, had told his story before; his voice had a certain narrative assurance. Yet his eyes had not lost an expression of dread as he remembered again, and perhaps his face would always wear the expression of terrified knowledge that death could come abruptly to a healthy young fellow like himself as it had to Potha. "He was well when he went to bed. I talked to him. There was nothing the matter. Then about midnight I heard him cry out."

"What kind of cry?" They had been over this in the reports and documents.

"Not a loud cry, a sort of whimper, soft and surprised. His eyes like this." The eyes of Sridor became as round as the eyes of evil spirits portrayed on the temple doors. His friend had cried out, opened his eyes round, and died. The light had faded from his face as Sridor watched, as if a ghost had come for him. It seemed as if he had seen something in his sleep or upon waking. Other boys had died like this, and people said it was the widow ghost wanting to marry the boy. Sridor's fingernails were painted red to trick the widow ghost into thinking he was a woman so she would let him alone.

"These deaths have happened among Southeastern Asian immigrants in a number of places," J. told me. "It has a number of names—in Japan it's *pokkuri*, in the Philippines it's called *bangungut*, somewhere it's *nonlaitai*, something like that, but it always means the same thing, sudden death at night, usually affects only males. We're calling it SUDS, sudden unexpected death syndrome."

Since I did not approve of cheerful acronyms for grim events, I said nothing. I was setting out glasses, as the other members of the council were coming to the Raffles Hotel for drinks before the banquet.

They sat uncomfortably propped against the headboards of the beds or on the luggage bench, discussing the strange disease.

"In my view some curious electrical cardiac accident," Randy Deckhorne said. "The path reports show no real cardiac defects, except surprising heaviness. The hearts weigh more than you would expect in chaps with slight builds."

"Well, that's by definition a cardiac abnormality," Don Harmon said. "Male hearts usually weigh less than four hundred grams of body weight, and these weigh considerably more."

"The symptoms are like shoshin beriberi," objected Dr. Kora. "I think a defect of the thiamine."

"Thymus," corrected Narcisse Cosset.

"A thiamine deficiency, he means," interpreted J.

"Yes," said Dr. Kora.

"Yes, I agree," said Dr. Cosset. *"Leur nourriture* is very bad, only a poor-quality rice."

"The issue of *Pseudomonas pseudomallei* hasn't been resolved," said J.

But it was clear to all the doctors that the young men had died of lonesome despair—thin-shouldered young men in ironed shirts huddled in foreign bars far from anyone who loved them, far from the happy jokes in their villages. Here in Singapore they were used to build the roads and the hideous shopping malls, and in the evenings sheltered in these shacks and maybe poisoned themselves by cooking their rice in plastic tubes. These deaths also happened among the Hmong from Laos when they went to Texas, among Kampucheans—always when away from home, always young men, lonesome and sad, the victims of the builders of shopping malls. As I emptied ice cubes from the minibar into the plastic bucket, I listened to the talk about the weight of the hearts of the young men. It seemed natural that their hearts would be heavy. The malls were made of glass and marble, as shining with brass as an English pub, as fountained as Versailles, fuller of Lacoste, Lanvin, Lauren, than department stores in Paris and New York, and wares from a thousand Asian basement factories, and gold, and silk, umbrellas, pens, crocodile bags, Rolexes.

It was not a watch you could wear in China. The gold, though fake, glittered too derisively in the blue-clad crowd, in the dun-colored dusty streets. The cheerful simplicity of the caps and sweaters, the battered bikes, the plastic shoes and absence of any finery pronounced such an object vulgar beyond vulgarity, ideologically disastrous, disgusting. Despising myself, I put it away in the little toilet kit the airline had passed out, out of sight, not wanting to tempt, or rather, not wanting to offend, the serious young man who brought the Thermos of hot water each morning, or the maid who set everything straight on the dresser. I grew fond of Chinese objects instead—the little plastic tube of Peacock dentifrice, the tin box with chrysanthemums stenciled on, the plastic combs and heavy stockings.

Now here it was again. If in China I had come to feel rather ashamed of having wanted it, now I was glad to see it. Some people, I have heard, are free from the impulse to keep souvenirs. I guess I am not. I like to have things that remind me of people and places—nothing as vulgar as a pillow that said BEIJING, or swizzle sticks in the shapes of women, but some private symbol of a place or event, and something you can't get at home. This is getting harder and harder. The baskets in the market in Arusha can also be found in San Francisco Imports Emporium. The linens are the same in Chinatown here as in China itself. Although one hoped for as a souvenir the amusing, the rare object or the bargain, perhaps the point was the hunt itself—tracking Woon's shop through the jungle of Singapore shopping centers, with the watch as a trophy testifying to valor and success, as stuffed heads did for the people who hunted animals.

I asked Yan if she would like to wash, and showed her to her room. When she came out again, she had some folded newspaper clippings, which she passed across to me.

"You will see that your watch had a good effect for one person at least."

"Yes, tell me how it happens to be here." I did want to

hear. Obviously the porter or maid had found it, had turned it in—that in itself astonishing. Perhaps such honesty is only astonishing to an American?

"First the hotel delivered it to Dr. Wang." Dr. Wang was known to the hotel as the person responsible for our presence, had booked our room, exerting his influence to get us a good one. I could imagine the reproaches of the hotel manager: "Your people left something in their room. What a nuisance." I wondered if it was easy for the maid or porter to have handed it over. Had they despised the gaudy watch or wanted it? "They understood that Dr. Wang would know how to return it to you."

I unfolded the clipping, a news story from the pages of the *China Daily*, the English-language newspaper in Beijing. HOTEL REWARDS SMART THINKING read the headline.

Wa Weng was recently commended by the management of the Beijing Hotel for many extra hours of service and for his brilliant thinking. When a valuable watch was found in the papers ready to be emptied out from the rooms on his floor, it was not clear whose watch it could be. He tells the story:

"When I first saw the watch it was in an airlines bag, of plastic, such as they would give you on China Airlines, but this one said TWA. It is known that TWA is an American airplane, but the trouble was, the TWA does not fly into Beijing. So there was no clue there! Also in the airplane bag was a razor, a toothbrush and a little rag to polish shoes. Now here was a clue, for the little rag said Raffles Hotel, Singapore!

"Thus, it is likely that our guest had come from Singapore. Some conversation with a friend who works at the airport confirmed my guess, that only three air-

lines come from Singapore: China Airlines, Qantas, and
Singapore Airlines. Now we had something to go on! I
was able to suggest to my manager that he get in touch
with these three airlines, with the names of our guests
who had been there not more than three months, and
in time we would find the trail. The trail would lead
to Raffles Hotel, and TWA, and it would give us a
name! The name of the person who had flown to Singapore on TWA, and then stayed in Raffles Hotel and
then come here. But in my heart I thought it was
probably these certain Americans. From the timing of
the discovery, it must be people who had just left, I
reasoned, and two Americans had left that morning.
Also, the bracelet of the watch is very small, and the
American woman was smaller than most Americans.
Also, Americans would be likely to be on TWA."

When commending Weng, the Manager Yetsu Yan
noted that he will soon be given the job to be in charge
of the entire fifth floor, a rapid step up for a dedicated
worker.

"So you see, it was an instrument of fate for Weng Wa,"
Yan said. I was touched, but could not help but be embarrassed that so much effort had been gone to. I was glad that
at least the trouble I had put people to had produced a happy
result for the hotel man, Weng. The lives of people in China,
so many were there, hung on little accidents, chance prefer-
ments, anything to make you stand out from the others. I
remembered the bureau in our room, covered with visiting
cards given J. by dozens of young Chinese, each one hoping
to be noticed by J., to be allowed to study abroad, or to
travel, or even to be commended by J. to someone higher

up in China. Thinking of this made me remember something rather malicious I had done to one of them, a Dr. Fang.

One day while out walking, I had become aware that someone was following me. Looking back over my shoulder made me certain; one face in the approaching mass of faces halted and ducked when I looked around. I sensed as I faced ahead, walking quickly to keep pace with the quick walkers, the relevance of some certain footsteps behind me to my own pace, slowing when mine did. When I turned down a lane of low houses, someone else did too. I supposed it was some-one from the hotel—a spy, a security agent, someone mis-trusting me. This makes one feel curiously important. I stopped and whirled, to surprise him, but couldn't tell which it was among the people walking, dangling their plastic sacks or carrying briefcases or wheeling bicycles behind me. In China you cannot be alone, but no one would approach you either. Alone and not alone, among the billion, like a bean in a jar.

Once I had been asked to talk to a group of J.'s Beijing students about my work and life in America, and when I wrote my name on the blackboard, the group, usually so polite, had tittered. Why? Because I wrote with my left hand. Does no one in China write with his left hand? No, they said. And there is no Rh negative blood, J. told me. I am a compendium of recessive traits, but there were no recessives here. You had to be like everyone else right down to the genes.

Yet I was not, was conspicuously blue-eyed and Western, and someone was surely following me. As I turned again, this figure detached himself from the people in the lane and confidently advanced on me. Perhaps I had dropped some-thing, or left something at the department store? He looked familiar, in his forties perhaps, a pale, lemon-colored man, his eyes the tiniest slivers; his graying Fu Manchu beard, daintily stuck to the center of his chin, was several inches long, like a wisp of smoke trailing downward. Something frightening about him made me look down at myself, to see what I had lost or was missing, or what I had by me to ward him off with. Yet of course harm was unthinkable. There was no harm in China, unless you were a thief, and then they executed you in the football stadium, and were sometimes embarrassed when a tourist busload happened to spy the corpses. This had happened to a woman from Cincinnati, who had talked to me once in the bar of the Beijing Hotel.

As he approached, the man spoke. "Mrs. M.?" His voice had a thin, an artificial quality, as if produced mechanically, an imitation of a Western voice.

"Yes."

Still he advanced, drawing so close to me that I was obliged to step backward, and, as he stepped still closer, another step backward until I had backed into the mud wall of the house behind me. When he leaned toward me, I smelled his strange vinegar smell. I shrank; he placed his face close to mine, and whispered in my ear, his words dispersed by the intimate sibilance of his whisper. "Pssssss," I heard, as in a playground game. Perhaps this was a Chinese form of menace, like the kiss of the Mafia don. Perhaps it was the dreaded Chinese whisper. It was the middle of the day now, with people trudging by in this normal land, paying us no attention, so I did not scream. Instead I said loudly, "I'm afraid I didn't understand you."

"Pssssssss." Now I did make something out of the tickling hiss. "I am Dr. Fang," he was whispering. "Can you speak to Dr. M. for me? I want to go to work with him in America. I have written to him. But if you will speak to him—all will be well."

Finally understanding, I squirmed away from the man's insistent breath in my ear.

"You must speak to my husband yourself," I said.

"Tell him I will work very hard. I will help him. I want to learn."

Relieved of my fright, I could now attend to what I was hearing in his music-box voice, its urgent despair, its desperation.

"I will tell him I saw you," I said. "I'm sorry, I have to go."

"I have brought you this," he said, stuffing a package into my shopping basket. "Oh, thank you, thank you, dear lady," and without warning, before I could give him back the package, he leapt into a wave of oncoming people and was swept away with them.

In the hotel room, I opened the package, a green glass bird on a branch, meant to look like jade, I supposed, or was jade of some thick, dull, glasslike, inferior kind. We had been taken to see the jade carvers, young women sitting at benches. Their blocks of jade had numbers and lines drawn on them in ink, like a paint-by-numbers canvas, and they had only to work away according to the numbers, with their little, wheezing dentist's drills. Everywhere the whine of excavation and the gurgle of water gave the impression of being in a purgatory of dentists. J. had been upset at the thought of the lungs of the girls as they breathed the dangerous jade particles loosened in the air; he wrote, frowning, in his notebook. I minded the idea of the drudgery of these poor girls, not even allowed to make up their own designs.

"The master craftsmen make the designs," the factory manager had explained, proud of their industry.

"How sad. I find it sad that people should be confined like

that," I said crisply to the factory manager, who paid no attention.

This was now my punishment, to own this ugly product of the sweatshop, symbol as well of the desperation of Dr. Fang, his sacrifice. As I put it on J.'s dresser, with Dr. Fang's card, my eye fell on the array of other cards stacked there, Drs. Liu, Ma, Ron, Ree, Li, Chang, Cui, Zhang, Hum—these indistinguishable monosyllables my stupid Western brain couldn't assimilate rendering indistinguishable also their hopes, personal histories, their brilliance or beauty, charm or lack of it, each one trying to stand out for me, or rather, for J. It was J. they wanted, they wanted jobs in his laboratory, they wanted training, wanted travel, wanted escape or some chance at small Western comforts, or whatever it was they did want, showering J. with cards, with presents he couldn't refuse and they couldn't afford, saving up to bring these ugly lacquer teacups, this embroidered kitten chasing a butterfly. This young man, whose card was on top, I remembered because of his Western first name—Roderick. They chose their Western names from a book, I had heard, or got them from some exchange student who mischievously called them Lionel or Marvin.

I wondered what Dr. Fang's first name might be. Wun Fang. Long Fang. Dam Fang. I felt sorry for him, but I hated him because of the intimate way he had whispered into my ear, his breath making its way inside it, like someone blowing into a shell, a rape of my ear. I imagined him saying boastfully, "I had the ear of Dr. M.'s wife." I imagined palace eunuchs whispering in the ears of courtiers. Perhaps whispering was the normal medium of Chinese intrigue.

When I showed J. the jade bird, I didn't tell him about the insult to my ear.

"He must be desperate," I said.

"They're all desperate, for more training. It's the way to success here. They all want to come to America."

And later, when we were ready to leave, J. had turned over the cards on his bureau, trying to remember which one went with which face, which life, and asking me if I remembered this person or that, and when he said "Fang Won?" I had said nothing, had pretended not to remember him, when he was the one I remembered best.

Now I asked, continuing our conversation about China, if Yan had news of Dr. Fang.

"Oh, poor Dr. Fang," she said. "Not really. He did not succeed in coming to America as he had hoped, that I know. Instead he was sent to Shenyang, in the North. I think he was a little too old to profit from study in America. Some people have lost time during the Cultural Revolution. I think he had hoped to be the one to bring you your watch. I saw his letter to Dr. Wang." In her face I could just discern, now, the satisfaction of someone compliant and reliable who knows she is in good standing. She might even, from her sly little smile, have done something to hasten the exile of Dr. Fang.

"What would you like to do while you're here?" I asked. "I'll begin by showing you around the neighborhood." I was going to say "Chinatown," which is the name of our neighborhood, but suddenly wondered if that would be taken as racist. But why should it be? "This is a Chinese area, in fact, so you'll see many things to remind you of home."

I was not prepared, though, for Yan's reaction as she and I walked along Grant Avenue, looking at the Chinese grocery stores and souvenir shops, and stacks of soybean casks, and ducks hanging, and Chinese people in padded gray coats jostling and feeling the fruit at the vegetable stall. Her reaction was one of joy. Her face glowed, and she looked around her almost with hunger, her eyes shining. "How beautiful it is, it is like China!" she cried again and again.

Now I saw that tears were standing in Yan's eyes. Of course she must be homesick, she had been nine months in Houston already, and would be away from China five years altogether—the time it would take for a Ph.D. in biochemistry. Chinese stayed away for even longer sometimes, lacking the money to go home again, or afraid to go back. Sometimes their child grew up without them. Even women left their children, had to leave them. I remembered all this as I walked with Yan, in her permanent so unsuitable for Chinese hair, and the ugly clothes from the Wangfujing department store, finery she must have saved up for, and the stout shoes so unsuitable for a girl her age—in her midtwenties, probably, with the little hands and rounded cheeks of a doll.

We had lunch in the New Asia Dim Sum Parlor. I asked Yan to order. "It's in Cantonese. I can't really speak Cantonese," she apologized. "Though of course I can read the menu." I nodded encouragingly at each selection and tried to suggest that we needed another. She ordered five dishes, looking shyly at me.

Over her ginger chicken she said, "I did not know America was like this. I thought it was all like Houston." I had never been to Houston, but I could imagine it—freeways, skyscrapers, the life of the automobile. How horrible it must seem to someone used to footpaths and bicycles and trees in leaf overhead, and the pretty tiled roofs. "I am so relieved for America, that some of it is nice," she said. Clearly her view of it had been as a horrible place, violent, made of cement, its dark, overbearing buildings with windows like mirrored sunglasses, eyes invisible, rendering its soul indecipherable and menacing. America doesn't inevitably strike people as wonderful. You often hear of people coming to America with joyful hearts, to find only the chill of air-conditioning in high-rise buildings, or the cockroaches of transient hotels. In addition to physical discomforts, their hopeful dreams of betterment are taken from them here.

Yan had a new American name, Iris, she said. She told me about her life in Houston, at the Baylor University medical school. Her days consisted of working in the hospital laboratory, then going to the library to study. She studied medical textbooks, English, biochemistry, and microbiology. She ate in the hospital dining room, and at night made tea for herself in her dormitory room. She studied until after midnight every night. There were one or two other Chinese students, but it was a bleak and solitary life, driven by something I knew I could never understand. It was too late for people like us to feel those passions for study, for excellence, for struggling to climb up to a safe spot.

When traveling, I had often thought of how it must be to be stuck far from home, displaced, alone, lying in a room. In every place I have visited I have seen some despised and lonesome person from another place—usually a man, for it seems to be the men who are extra, who are sent off, like the Chinese men who built the California railroad, or the migrant Mexicans in their tin barracks, lascars, solitary Turks in Munich, little Algerians so proudly male in North Africa, so invisible and despised in France. If you are a woman displaced you go on being a woman, but men lose the advantage of being men, and become dark personages glimpsed in restaurant kitchens or wearing fluorescent vests as they sweep the gutters, the bright colors seeming to ask that people see them, and yet no one does. Surely it is harder for men than for women—unless you are a boat person, adrift, captured by pirates to be raped and drowned. Far from home, men were reduced, resourceless, and lonely. Sentiment over-came them. They gathered in bars or squatted on dusty curbings. Yugoslavs in chilly England, Israelis in New York, forlorn Ethiopians or Nigerians selling ballpoint pens in Paris or Milan, alone in their blackness, away from their mothers, miserable with cold.

At the close of the meal, as I was mechanically opening my fortune cookie, which said, "A happy surprise will reward you," Yan drew a long envelope from her purse.

"I wonder if I can ask you to talk about something to Dr. M. for me," she said.

"Of course," I said, but vaguely, trying to read upside down the papers that Yan unfolded and smoothed out. She put them in front of me.

"These are some papers which an American must sign to sponsor a Chinese student. I am sponsored by my advisor at Baylor, but I am full of hope that my twin sister could come to America too, and Dr. Hunter, my advisor, cannot sponsor two people. It would be no trouble, and no expense. She will live in my room with me, and I have a grant that will be enough for us both. I know that the paper makes you promise to pay for us, but that would not be necessary. See, I have filled out all the details, all Dr. M. would have to do is sign." I saw the hope on Yan's face, the trustful expectation of a positive reply. She would make a sacred promise, she continued to explain, that her sister Ran would not do any-thing to make us ashamed, or cause us fear or inquietude. Dr. Hunter would have been happy to do it, but he could not, and since she knew she would be seeing Dr. and Mrs. M., in connection with the valuable watch, she had dared to hope . . .

I reassured her that I would speak to J., adding, however, that he had a fear of forms and papers and might not like it.

I would do what I could. I had in fact to pick up J. at the airport that afternoon. Would Yan come? But Yan said she would stay to walk in Chinatown.

I was relieved, for I could imagine that J. would balk at the idea of becoming sponsor to an unknown Chinese twin. He would imagine debts, midnight phone calls, security deposits, complaints from landladies. But he agreed, even rose to the occasion, signing with great affability, after dinner. Yan's face flushed with relief. She left the room to put the signed papers safely in her luggage. I knew that this had been her purpose in coming, explaining the unusual luxury of her spending money on a plane fare from Houston to San Francisco. Except for needing these papers signed, Yan would have gone on thinking that all America was like Houston, whatever Houston was like.

I found myself thinking of Dr. Fang's glass bird, so I had a look in the china cupboard and found it. I was relieved. It would have been like me to throw it out, and now it seemed important to have it, a little flame keeping alive the recollection of poor Dr. Fang, and to remind me of the arbitrary operation of bad luck, that he should have whispered in my ear, and of my thoughtless cruelty. When Yan had gone to bed, I wrote the letter to Dr. Wang, thanking him for my watch and apologizing for the trouble I had put them all to. My words had the ring to me of the false contrition of self-criticism, yet they were sincere.

Power Structures

*As an Englishman does not travel to see Englishmen, I re-
tired to my room.*

LAURENCE STERNE

It came as a shock—as a calculated insult or criticism, after
the luxury of Cairo, and after the Egyptians' kindness to us,
to be put up in a sinister hotel like this. We felt puzzled
and wounded at first, especially J., who had thought he was
helping them, and took it even as a punishment. Eventually
it made us examine our easy expectations of comfort and
indulgence. But at the moment the issue was how to escape.
Of course it was impossible to stay. There were the smells
of Nile silt, diesel fuel, and camel dung, the flies and mosquitoes swarming in at a broken screen, the fetid puddle on
the floor of the cement shower, with streaks of rust running
down the metal side walls as if someone had been murdered
in it. Two sagging beds were pushed foot to foot along the
stained wall, repellent camp blankets pulled over doughlike
pillows, a rime of mildew; it brought to mind interrogation
cells, Latin torture, disappearance—these associations all too
easy to arrive at because of why we were here—at the behest
of the Egyptian military. That sounded sinister on the face
of it. The General. "We're all generals here," Dr. Hafez had
said. But why had they put us in a hotel like this?

Our resolution to leave, just to stalk out, animated our
anxiety; surely we would be prevented. The secret agenda,
whatever it was, would become manifest. Until now it had
all been seeming too wonderful, in a country where things

were not wonderful. Maybe people disappeared in Luxor. Maybe we had fallen into the hands of a rival faction, the people who had murdered Sadat, or maybe the Israeli secret service. All this preposterous but the effect of the hotel, and the rapid fall of our fortunes.

We had arrived in Cairo the month before, J. to aid in setting up some programs against infectious disease with the Egyptian army—the body entrusted with public health in Egypt. Thus the generals—plump, amiable doctors with Islamic mustaches, in beige uniforms by day, dark business suits for restaurants at night, with pleasant, French-speaking wives, or Western wives, often nurses married during their training in London or Arizona or Rochester. The wife of General Hafez was a Scottish nurse, rawboned and cheerful, and the wife of General Bilawi was a tiny redhead named Scherzad.

The power of the generals was evident in the splendor of our arrangements—first-class airfare (but it had to be on Air Egypt, and everything had to be Islamic: "If you want a drink before dinner, you have to take along a little gin in a flask," the English travel agent had advised). A comfortable suite at the Meridien. The Meridien is a French hotel, owned by Air France, and its restaurants were directed by a famous French chef with no Islamic influence on the wine list.

So we had passed three weeks in Cairo. J. would work with the generals—and a part of his work consisted in consulting, after hours, on the cases of their wives and aunts with coughs, and the ailing children of politicians. "I can't tell them much they don't know already," J. said. It seemed to be the novelty or prestige of having a foreign doctor that drew them.

At the end of the afternoons, a few hours were reserved for sightseeing, to the pyramids or, over and over again, to

the wondrous museum, whose treasures—the staring sarco-
phagi and tiny mummies of cats, and golden-footed chairs—
endlessly drew us, or we just drove in the teeming streets,
and in the evening went to some balmy restaurant, perhaps
on the bank of the Nile, open to the night air, for roast
pigeon in honey.

We had been unprepared for the glorious pyramids of
Cheops, Cheophren, and Menkaru, so familiar from childhood, from the dollar bill and ads for Camel cigarettes, and
from the whole idea of pyramidness. We were overcome by
their unspoiled and austere beauty, the sight of them rising
in the desert as from the sands of time, though they were
really in a suburb of Cairo. They endured the assaults of the
son et lumière without losing their strangeness and dignity.
Claustrophobic, I did not stand in line to go into the excavated chambers, but waited outside, hectored by the would-
be guides and money changers, thinking of the builders and
servants of the ancient pharaohs who had had to remain in
there with the mummies of their royal masters, hearing the
great stones slide closed according to the secret mechanisms,
immuring them for all time; I hoped this would not happen
to J. I am afflicted with a poor sense of historical perspective;
what happened in the ancient world seems to me not so long
ago and could happen again, some stone accidentally pushed
and set in motion, the huge slabs silently dropping into the
ancient tracks, sealing off J.

In the mornings, in the hotel room, I worked at writing
a novel—a novel set in Persia, as it happened—and would
go out alone to refresh my memory with the present sights
of Cairo, the veiled women and donkey carts, the modest
billboards with their beautiful calligraphy, the ruined colonial buildings still imposing with laundry hung out on the
porches, the whole city oddly sumptuous and elegant. My

research presented some problems—the main problem for a woman who wanted to walk to the museum or to any of the other tourist spots or who wanted to shop, or just to idle along the streets, to view the life there. The problem was the little men. Although plenty of women were evident on the streets—secretaries on their lunches, women shopping, women pushing children in prams—a foreign woman would be beset by scores of little men of all ages, uniformly thin, dark, desiccated as if left out in the sun, wearing greasy round caps, their stained, shabby suits neatly brushed. Each of these, even the little boys, even the oldest men, must have been the sole support of a houseful of women, an infinitude of children. What else could explain their desperate persistence, the ingenuity of their scams as they fastened themselves on Western tourists, sticking like doppelgängers that could not be shaken. Alongside they walked, proffering repulsive souvenirs, demanding that you buy "the genuine" piece of mummy cloth, tomb figure, piece of lace or embroidery, banner reading EGYPT, or RAMSES, ancient pot or potsherd, T-shirt, unguent, charm—"psst, lady, found in a tomb . . . five thousand years old . . . do you need a guide?" This chorus of presentation, the frenzy of their hopes, the stridor of their competition howled in the ears as if you were in purgatory. Confident of the power of any man over any woman, sometimes they employed terror techniques, claiming to have been hired by me, or affronted—"you hired me, lady, and now you must pay; you came down this street and you have to pay; there is a charge, there is a fine." Sometimes they pushed one another to be the one to render some unwanted service, and ended by scuffling and falling in the dust.

One step outside the compound of the Meridien, where first it was necessary to shake off the cries of the drivers leaning on their cars, and the boys and little men like the dogs in Rabelais came bounding from everywhere, stifling the walker with the mixture of their sweat, perfume, tobacco—for all smoked endlessly, little wet, crabbed cigarettes rolled by hand. A black dress and head scarf did something to mitigate this, but not if you were spotted leaving the hotel. Another dilemma was sunglasses—if you didn't wear them, the bright Mediterranean light hurt your eyes; your blue eyes gave you away. If you wore them, you were a foreigner on the evidence of it, or at least rich. It came to me that the gnarled, old faces—the faces so full of what we call character—on people in Greece, in Egypt, in any bright, hot place, were so from a lifetime of squinting against the fierce sun. Or something in my gait gave me away—what it was I never found, but I never could fool the Egyptian pursuers. I pitied their frantic pleas but hated them too, for plaguing my dreamy excursions when I wanted to moon over the caskets of the pharaohs, or wander on the banks of the Nile. Our driver, Yusef, taught me the words for "sorry," "no," and "go away," but to little avail.

J. had asked the general if it was dangerous for a woman to walk on the streets of Cairo. "Of course not," he said. "Egyptians are good people, or anyway they are too lazy to make trouble."

Yet Yusef's car had an unmarked license, and he didn't wear a uniform. Years ago in Guatemala, before anyone was aware of troubles there, we had noticed that the private houses had armed guards outside them. Our friend had said, "Oh, no, there's no danger, it's just a kind of prestige thing, a form of conspicuous consumption." Three times, in three countries, on mild summer days when no danger was predicted, a scene of police, and revolutionary violence has erupted in a peaceful street before my eyes—this lends to travels an only provisional sense of security and always the knowledge that you can't really understand what's going on, not even the people who live there can, and if anything it is they who underestimate the danger. "It's perfectly safe if you know what you're doing," people will say who live in New York or Detroit or Beirut. But familiarity has dampened their sensors.

"The voucher," J. suddenly said, in the disgusting Luxor hotel room. "The travel thing, the papers—the guy has them." It was true that we had given our guide the papers the general had given us. "This will see to your hotel, and the plane trip to Aswan from Luxor, and all the things you will need in Luxor," the general had said, and we had given away these papers to the man who had met us at the Luxor airport.

The Egyptians are proud of their magnificent monuments—the Valley of the Kings, Aswan, the fabulous columned temple at Karnak—and had wanted to be sure we had time to enjoy them. Part of J.'s arrangements therefore included a visit to Luxor and Aswan. Yusef had driven us to the airport, we had made the short flight. A throng of sweating guides and screaming taxi drivers pressed toward the passenger exit to snatch the hesitant tourists who descended in Luxor. We were not sure how to identify the person we had been told would meet us, but he identified us. "Mister," he said, seizing my case.

"Arab Travel Services?" J. consulted the papers again, though he had looked at them on the plane.

"Yes, yes, come with me." We were soon in his battered car, and then put down at the peeling hotel. No, no mistake, he said, this was the hotel, they were expecting us.

We would walk somewhere, find another hotel, there must be a Hilton or something. We couldn't see that it mattered about the voucher; we ourselves would just pay for the few days at another hotel. Anything would be better than staying here. J. picked up our suitcases, and we braced ourselves for the unpleasant confrontation in the lobby when we announced we were leaving.

We were right in all this. The manager, at J.'s grim countenance as he handed back the key, began to remonstrate before he even heard our explanation. But we were polite, we were firm. To ourselves we earnestly hoped that our ingratitude in leaving would not somehow get back to the general, and we fled into the dusty street, tottering under our cases, sweating in the heat of the late afternoon. Rude, unreliable Americans, too finicky to accept the kindnesses they were given, we supposed they were saying.

There was of course another hotel, unexceptionable, built for the boatloads of tourists who came off the Nile cruises to shower on dry land at last, spend the night, attend the *son et lumière* at Karnak and visit the Valley of the Kings. Without exception, the ones we talked to in the bar in the evening complained that Nile cruises are unbearably boring. Our informants were mostly well-prepared English tourists who knew the dates of the Middle Kingdom and the particulars of the reign of Amenhotep, condemned to drink gallons of beer day after day as the boats slunk along the brown, slimy banks, staring at the villagers busy with their daily lives who did not bother to stare back.

Near Luxor we saw the temple of Karnak, imposing indeed; its giant columns and vast courts impressed on us the mightiness of the Ramseses, and also how enduring were the hatreds of the region. High above our heads the undimmed friezes showed Egyptians fighting Assyrians, Syrians, Persians, Armenians, Ethiopians, Hittites, and numberless other tribes, some now vanished, some with unfamiliar names, and most still extant and still fighting. With appropriate emotions of awe we strolled in lanes of crouching sphinxes and rams strung with electrical cords and loudspeakers.

The mystery of our demotion continued to trouble us. I wondered what sin of forward Western wife I might have committed. J. brooded back over the various private patients the generals had brought to him, wondering if there had been a complaint, an error. He thought particularly of one, a boy, nephew of the general's sister-in-law, bronchitic, his little chest already the pouter pigeon breast of an old smoker, doomed in the dust of Cairo, to whose parents J. had said, "You must take him away," only then seeing, as they regarded him with forlorn, deep icon eyes, the impossibility of going away anywhere. Or there was the wife, with the fashionable yellow-orange hair, who had had to wait for several hours because the generals, unconcerned that a woman had to wait, had kept him in the field. But none of this seemed sufficient to explain the sudden withdrawal of their largess. A more cynical explanation was, of course, that since J. had finished his work with them, they had no further use for us.

In the hot morning, crossing the Nile on a barge with a thousand others toward the Valley of the Kings, we saw that the Arab tourist agent, the one with our vouchers, was following us. He did not approach us, but neither did he hide, he only sat watching us from a position in the stern of the ferry, and seemed to think himself invisible to us, in his brightly striped shirt, staring boldly but not acknowledging our glances at him. Probably he was there in connection with his duties as a tourist agent, guide to someone else, in charge of a party of people, but he made us uncomfortable, so we went astern to watch the receding shore of Luxor with the imposing ruins of Karnak visible behind us.

In the Valley of the Kings we forgot for a while our tormentor in the excitement of stepping into the excavated chambers of the royal tombs of vanished pharaohs and their ministers and wives, choosing our moment between the arrival of groups of tourists speaking numberless languages. The bare, swept tombs gave in their darkness the idea of death restful and long. The hieroglyphic pictures traced along the upper courses of brick the stories of life after death, with figures glaring walleyed at us as they marched sideways around the tomb in their little sarongs, carrying offerings of fish and grapes. The colors, ocher and blood-dark crimson, were the same as on the tombs of the ancient Mayas, and the Greeks, and perhaps on all the monuments of antiquity, now so gleaming and bare.

We strolled through the tumbled ruins of palaces and temples, and across meadows of parched grass littered with tumbled stones and pillars. I have never been able to cure myself of the hope that ruins that have been scoured for eons by the generations of humans picking them over will magically yield one more fragment. I stumble along peering at my feet, missing the birds and the cloud formations, hoping for an ancient stone that on closer inspection will prove to have a tiny face carved on it, or to be an ax or arrowhead, or a piece of a statue. No doubt this is everyone's hope. People do find things, but I am not one, too myopic, and not lucky at it. I have a friend, a painter, whose eye better perceives the shape of things, perceives the immanent form—he found a stone ax on a forest path in the Midi. When I was a child, my friends often found arrowheads in the ravines of our Illinois village; looking down I would see only earthworms and spring beauties and the odd gum wrapper. So we stumbled over the clean-swept rubble of the Valley of the Kings, waiting behind tourist lines to enter the tomb of

Thutmose or Petamen-apt, me looking down, J. looking ahead, or, occasionally, behind, and so announced that the man was still following us.

"We must have been put in that hotel so he could watch us," J. said. "It doesn't make any sense." Luxor, flooded with tourists, of whom we were only two more, as innocent of political objectives as the Iowans in their tennis shoes and baseball caps crowding in at the entrance to the Ramesseum. Why would anyone watch us?

We had started early, according to the best advice, before the midday sun at this hot season, but there was so much to see that we had skipped lunch, and by midafternoon were ourselves ruined and parched, numbed by the size of the vast columns and mighty stones everywhere in the gray grass. J., with his sure instinct for the sources of beer, saw nestled at the back of a temple a little restaurant where one might get a cold drink, and we went in. It seemed to me that I could see our man following at some distance, outside the square opening of a tomb. He appeared to us everywhere, like a hallucination.

The restaurant was nearly empty, obviously off the tourist itinerary, a mud-floored room of cement block that smelled dank, a fact that seemed peculiar in a desert, but made it at least alluringly cool; and there was a pleasant-looking patio beyond, shaded by a straggling vine on an overhead trellis. Two other tables of people instantly fell silent as we came in, as if we had surprised some nefarious negotiation. As the man had made us already apprehensive, this made us feel even more so, but we were grateful to be out of the heat.

We ordered. At the table behind J., two men began to speak again, in French, but the larger party, across the patio, still sat in constrained-looking silence, darting us covert looks and overt stares. Three men and two women, one of these very fat. I would have said from their clothes they were all Americans, except for the fat woman, whose olive skin and black hair made her possibly Egyptian. The youngest of the men was squat and overweight, the other had a pleasant, mobile face, like a comedian. The remaining man and woman, whom I took by their resemblance to each other to be a couple, were thin, refined-looking people with straight backs, perhaps in their sixties, slender and elegant in L. L. Bean clothes. There was something unlikely about the group, with their differing clothes and differing manners, a chance encounter of travelers who would be ill-assorted at home.

J. gave the waiter paper money, to which the man objected. "Coin, coin," he repeated, pointing at the next table until we understood. J. approached the two Frenchmen to ask for change. *"Avez-vous la monnaie?"* and they made change for him.

This little transaction in French seemed to relieve the group at the other table, who again began to speak, in loud, oblivious American voices. Their conversation amazed us into silence—mine the professional eavesdropping of a writer, and J.'s the indignation of an idealistic American citizen.

"Jesus Christ," said the fat man. "You never know, they might have been constituents. They turn up everywhere. Remember at the Kahala Hilton? A woman there sat near us on the beach, turned out to be a bleeping novelist, wrote down every word we said, and published it in the *Washington Post*."

The man who looked nicer said, "Luckily we're politicians, we don't actually say anything much."

The fat woman laughed. "Unfortunately Bert had said— we were visiting a naval base—that the commander, who was a woman, had a face like a whore."

"Luckily she was not a Florida voter," the fat man went

on. "Hey, anyway it wasn't an insult. Lots of my constituents are whores."

"Not to mention ourselves," said the nicer man. (Laughter.)

"I wish we were at the Kahala right now," the woman said. "I don't know about Egypt. For one thing, they're not even Jewish." (Laughter.) "No, but seriously, look at this place! This is your typical Egypt. Smells like donkey pee and there's nothing to eat."

"I do think the tombs are fascinating," said the other woman, a little anxiously, in a pleasant southern voice.

"Yes, I've always been fascinated by Egypt," her counterpart agreed.

"Oh, yes, fascinating," the fat woman agreed. "Absolutely. I just think a little foreign aid could be applied to their hotels."

"Listen, hon, look at it this way," said the fat man. "It's going to look incredibly accountable only spending forty bucks a night, anything to save the taxpayers' money."

"We don't even mention that there's no hotel for fifty," put in the nicer man, in an earnest way.

"We have the plane down here; in my opinion we should just fly back to Cairo," sniffed the fat woman.

As the conversation continued in this vein, we continued to be stricken with the chagrin any traveler feels when meeting up with countrymen who are vulgar and loud—for one is never such a snob as when traveling. But our shame was deepened by the realization that these were junketing American congressmen, at least one of them from Florida—I was eventually able to work out who they were—and they were all unaccountably talking like stage politicians, mocking their voters and Egypt with equal contempt.

The two Frenchmen, sitting behind J., had been looking

at us, it seemed sympathetically. At first I thought they must be amused at our embarrassment, that these other Americans could be so noisy and unattractive. But then I realized that, unless we looked it in some way, they couldn't know that we were American, for we hadn't said a word in English. (It is true that I was wearing Nikes—inevitable sign of female American tourist.) I hoped they hadn't understood, as we had, that these were our elected representatives.

The older couple, who had spoken very little, now rose. The woman tied a straw hat over her fair, graying hair, they gathered their stack of guidebooks, and ceremoniously took their leave. "Back to the serious sightseeing." The woman smiled. "We'll see you back at the hotel."

"Bye, Mrs. Serious," said the fat woman in a mocking voice, when the couple were out of earshot. "Bye bye, Senator."

"They aren't so bad, Maisie," said the other man. "They're very nice people, and he's smart, despite his out-to-lunch manner."

"I suppose. It's her I can't stand," said the fat woman. "A stuck-up goy."

Now the two Frenchmen stood up. *"Au revoir, Jacques,"* said one. When Jacques had left his companion, he approached us. *"Vous n'etes pas Français?* No? I didn't think so." His accent was English. "May I join you? Let me buy you another beer." At this the congressmen were in their turn struck as silent as the pyramids. Perhaps they had believed themselves unintelligible in a restaurant full of French people. I was vengefully glad for their discomfort—their stupidity and malice had blighted my idea of Congress, though I am sure we should not have been surprised. "Please join us, sure, sit down," said J. in his unmistakably American voice. He introduced us, adding, loudly, "From Fort Lauderdale."

Our new acquaintance was an English archaeologist who worked for the Louvre. Perhaps it gets boring, being on a long dig with the same people, for he clung to us so resolutely that J. began to look a little pensive. I imagined that he was thinking again of our sense that we were being watched.

"There are a lot of things to see just near here," said this new friend. "Would you like me to walk around with you for a little while? I'll show you the vocal Memnon, a statue from whom the voice of Memnon was last heard in the time of Hadrian."

Outside the restaurant, our man could be seen. Perhaps he was not the same man, some trick of our eyes, or of the desert light making Egyptians look alike. Yet he had the same crocheted cap, the same immutable grip on his prayer beads, and, in a landscape of tourists, looked only at us. We were never to learn why.

"I'm not sure I handled the general's brother's mother-in-law right," said J. miserably. "Nothing the matter with her at all, but maybe I shouldn't have said so in a way that contradicted the general—he'd been giving her a placebo . . ."

"I'll show you Ozymandias," said the archaeologist. "You remember Shelley's poem? 'Look on my Works, ye Mighty, and despair'? His 'shattered visage' is just a hundred yards from here." I wondered if the congressmen had seen it.

White Hunter

At first it had seemed okay, morally speaking, to have come. For J. to have come, at least. In my mind, doctors were exempt (like the Red Cross), could go places other people boycotted and protested. It was understood they were there to help people. As for me, since I had no serious excuse for being there—no journalistic mission, no relatives—my own presence in South Africa couldn't be justified apart from my role as J.'s companion. But I could be there as a witness. My role was to know. So that when the Jeep driver who had been taking us around the game park (a gentlemanly kid in shorts and army boots) did, on the third day, suddenly say, "They are more like animals than people, you know," I was there to hear it. "The natives here are," he continued. "The African. He even smells different. You can't teach him anything. He is like a child: he can't plan ahead. You give him a sack of peas and tell him it has to last him for the winter, it will be gone in a week all the same, then he will come back to you for more." I had been glad I was there to hear it. Forever after I would know, in discussions about South Africa, that the things that were said about the white people were true: they did despise and hate the blacks and talk insensitively. At least the Afrikaners did. In Capetown we had met many concerned, white English-speaking people, usually in the Jewish community, who were working for change. If nothing else, the traveler learns that things are rarely morally obvious.

This driver, Dirk, had only spoken out after three days. Before that the talk had been, with J., of birds, of the hundreds of species, and of the big animals we were seeing. Only after three days did he speak his mind, but now I knew his mind, the mind of South Africa. It reminded me of nothing so much as the mind of America, insofar as I had known the mind of America when I was little (about ten, in my small town), and people had said the same things about Indians—Native Americans—about how they couldn't plan ahead, couldn't drink, couldn't be trusted to look after themselves, couldn't be trusted period.

The little lodge we had stayed in also reminded me of my childhood, of camping in national parks built by the CCC, with the same dusty paths and green paint, the rangers wearing the same clothes as this young man, and the flag on its pole, and the faded map in its glass case, the families in their cars, with guidebooks and Thermos bottles. The families were all white here, of course, but then they had been all white in my childhood, too, families in their Chevys, children sitting in the dusk on the logs around the campfire area, unpacking their dolls. In America you could get out of your car. Here in South Africa a rather exciting air of menace and fortification was conveyed by the closing of the gates at dusk, and by the signs telling people to stay in their cars. The children in such an atmosphere, of course, stayed in the cars, or safely inside the lodge. Blond children, sturdy blond overweight parents—these the Afrikaners—and the English-speaking families, large-toothed and thin-legged in shorts, with binoculars.

The gates of this compound were shut each night against wild animals, not against the natives. J. and I had remarked on the general absence of anxiety in South Africa, the lack of security checks and metal detectors on the plane flying up here from Johannesburg. Across my mind the newsreels of the sixties: the marches and German shepherds and whips, the fat man called Bull, men in helmets and epaulets and boots, and shadowlike black children skipping, and the mothers and fathers singing, and preachers walking among them, and the mood of elation.

We were here by mistake. J. had been invited to visit a black hospital in one of the Homelands, when, with five days left on our immutable airline tickets, our passage to that area was canceled. De Boerck had suggested a few days of game watching instead, first in the Kruger National Park, and then in an adjacent private hotel, luxuriously run by a fellow he knew. These changes in our plans had put J. in a bad mood; he would rather have stayed in Tanzania; alternatively, there was a meeting in Nairobi he should have gone to. He does not support changes in plan very well.

Still, I couldn't shake off the feeling that I was in America, and couldn't stop thinking there ought to be a lesson in that, if I could think what it was. I had been feeling like this the day before in the Land Rover, but then had seen a giraffe. There had been no giraffes in Mississippi. This was another land, of rhino and elephant. The Mississippi marchers were a caramel color, handsome and sturdy, but here in the shadows the blackness of the Africans was different. The thinness of their limbs and the glint of their eyes—like coins against the purple blackness of their skin—made them seem unrelated to the Americans. Here the people wound their bodies in beautiful striped cloth, and the slowness of their steps and the swaying gait were African, not American.

Contrasting with the serious, austere, Boy Scout–like atmosphere of the Kruger National Park, the Simba Private Hotel and Game Reserve was cozy, overdecorated with "taste-

ful" faded chintzes and hunting trophies and prints—photos
of the famous people who had stayed there. I recognized Jerry
Lewis holding a pair of antlers. Jalousies shaded a broad lobby
where fans swirled slowly on the ceiling, and the stuffed
heads were hung of members of all the species of animal J.
and I had met, and coatracks made of their antlers—the
twisted spirals, the forked, the branched, these menacing
appendages which had been rather unconvincing on the mild-
eyed living creatures who had bounded away from our vehicles
on their tiny hooves. It was unbearable to look at the walls
here.

The White Hunter, as I thought of him—the owner and
friend of De Boerck—was an Englishman named Reeves,
with a hale, alcoholic manner, stocky form, arms and legs
(in shorts) covered with a mat of curly reddish hair, and
something behind his eyes not so drunk as he seemed. The
place was run on the lines of a European hotel; you sat at
the same table for breakfast and dinner, and said good morning to all the other guests. Then there were game drives or
game walks—these last by special arrangement—lunch,
more game drives and game walks, and "sundowners" by the
river, when you were meant to drink gin and watch the
animals gather down by the river, if they did. The animals
were not so abundant here as in Tanzania, and the atmosphere
was different. Where they had roamed in their numbers in
Tanzania, here they were prized like valuable freaks, with a
carnival of people depending on them—the drivers of the
smart vans, the uniformed blacks who erected gaily scalloped
canopies over the lunch area and spread the cloths on the
folding tables brought out into the bush, the cooks, the boys
who carried sturdy pikes to protect the guests on the game
walks or to give the illusion that they needed protection.

Where the gentle Tanzanians were reading tracts by their

leader Nyerere, and asking themselves what their attitude to the bourgeois should be, South Africa was the last stand of colonial privilege. Ian, the driver, was a good-looking Rhodesian, recently demobilized after some years as a mercenary in Mozambique. This romantic profession had left traces on his handsome face—rugged squint-lines and scars of sunburns. He was a white soldier of Africa who seemed to feel that his present duty—driving American ladies in a Jeep, with only an Uzi to hand—was about as dangerous as anything else he had done. When he allowed us to alight to stand for a while concealed in a blind of thatch and bamboo, he guarded us alertly with the rifle in his arms. No game, however, menaced us. He granted us a short walk through the jungle underbrush, he walking in front. I was glad at last to walk. To be in Africa, like being in Alaska, is to be confined in some kind of motor vehicle every minute of every day.

Ian told us of the misery of Mozambique; the wandering women and dead babies, the endless dust. "Poor bloody bastards, they think they want freedom, there's not a place in Africa where the black man is better off than right here," he said.

"Of course the animals are protected," he said, adding in a lower tone, "though we might take someone hunting from time to time, by special arrangement." That would be his real job, I supposed, clandestine hunting trips with rich Americans or Germans. Looking at Ian's Uzi, I thought of Americans shooting buffalo from the trains moving west across the American plains and leaving their corpses where they fell. I thought of those rednecks in Florida who teach their children to hunt and kill baby deer.

"What do you hunt?" J. asked Ian.

"Well, antelope, that sort of thing," he said, looking off

into the underbrush, his tone unconvincing. He has killed elephants and lions, I thought. I imagined them loading tusks of contraband ivory in the night. What if your child grew up to be a mercenary? There was something of the gentleman about his accent, not as harshly South African as some, the vowels a little more English, an occasional complicated word betraying an elaborate education somewhere along the line.

From the grounds of the Simba Private Hotel and Game Reserve, Ian drove us back into the Kruger National Park. All the vegetation around here was more equatorial—lush and ferny—than the land farther north. The trees had soft, inviting leaves instead of the thorns of the Tanzanian trees, and flowers and trailing vines laced the branches overhead. A single tree groaned, half bent beneath the weight of an immense orchid plant in bloom, its petals of white and orange making it seem as if a million butterflies had landed in it. An African tree orchid, Ian said, was a rare, protected species. He said he hadn't realized there was one nearby.

At dinner, J. and I were almost alone in the dining room, except for the glass eyes of the glowering beasts whose stuffed expressions of perpetual ferocity I had found unsettling at breakfast. The White Hunter himself sat at a corner table talking to a woman with blond hair vaguely wiglike in its brightness. The White Hunter did not look at her, but instead scanned the room with his *sanpaku* eyes. *Sanpaku* is the word I had read somewhere to describe the kind of eyes in which you see the white below as well as above and to the side of the iris. It is a sign of bad health and can be remedied by eating brown rice. The bright-haired woman drank her Pym's cup, clutching it with both red-fingernailed hands. From the bar, we could hear the light laughter of a group of men. Black waiters in white jackets gave an air of seriousness to the bringing of pea soup, salad, a roast that seemed to have been boiled and tasted gamey, raising apprehensions about which sort of animal, among those pitiably decapitated creatures nailed on the wall, it had been.

We smiled at a couple like ourselves, a man and woman our age, and I marveled at how other women can turn themselves out—nails, coils of hair arranged with a maximum of intention—in the wilds of Africa. I have seen them do it anywhere. It means caring enough to lug a hair dryer along, or giving up the sightseeing of the afternoon to make an appointment with a hairdresser. Plenty of women are like that. My hair straggled, still damp from the shower, and my arm was spotted with mosquito bites, reminding me of my arms and ankles as a child—mosquitoes and the dreaded chiggers. In the meantime I had almost forgotten, until now, how it was to have a body all bitten and covered with sores, even though most of the people in Africa do, and India, and wherever you were on any of several subcontinents. Here we dutifully took our chloroquine and hoped for the best.

As I was thinking about insect bites, the waiter's hands suddenly intruded across our plates in white gloves, like the hands of a mime. In Spain we had had dinner once in a private house where the servants wore white gloves like this, a fastidiousness that had seemed a little disagreeable, implying the dirtiness of hands. And here it seemed to mean, no black hands, only white hands, are touching your food.

"Buffalo or maybe wild pig," J. said of the meat.

After dessert, the waiters detached from their brackets the tiki-torches that lighted the patio, and carried them nearer to the musicians who were gathering at one end of the dining room. From the direction of the kitchen a procession of women entered into the circle of light, and the drums adopted a pronouncedly African beat, excited and jungly, trying to suggest exhilarating savagery tattooed from village to village on hollow logs and gourd marimbas. The women had brightly colored kangas knotted around their waists and were topless. The flickering light of the torches, like the dappled light of an African forest, cast stripes and spots of shadow across their naked breasts. They were light colored or darkest black, were small and stocky or tall, willowy Ethiopians, and their breasts were all different— small, low, high, flat, pendulous; it was like a plastic surgeon's book of choices. One woman had the voluptuous fat breasts of a stripper and another a mere protrusion of nipple. The nipples were black against lighter skin or small, like the spots on cats.

These women began to dance, a dance consisting of standing in one place and bouncing up and down on first one and then the other foot, half bending and extending their knees, while making small dog-paddling motions with their arms in time to the drum music, which imperceptibly quickened. The compelling feature of the dance was simply breasts, jiggling up, down, up, down, to the drumbeat, faster and faster.

Now I noticed that these same women were the chambermaids during the day, recycled as danseuses. There was the girl who had made our bed this morning. Her expression was bored, or, more likely, tired. It was terrible to think that the poor girl, tired after the day, had to take her clothes off and jiggle up and down for tourists. I could hardly bear this, nor could I turn away. In the middle of this strange misery, J. stood up and tugged at my elbow. His look and the set of his shoulders expressed either his disgust at this exploitation of tired cleaning women made to bare their breasts for tourists at the end of a long day; disgust at the management's idea of us—tourists and Americans—thinking we would want to see the breasts of poor African chamber-maids; or maybe just boredom. I had never before walked out of anything, not even a movie, am compelled by temperament to sit transfixed until the bitter end of whatever it is. My heart pounded with excited indignation and relief as I followed J. out.

We heard footsteps behind us on the stair. I still felt irrational fear, as if, having seen something shameful or illicit, we would be pounced on or pierced from behind, as the tigers in India pounce on men in the forest. When I turned at the top of the stairs, I saw it was the Hunter himself.

"Not our cup of tea," J. said.

"I know," the Hunter said, smiling, blithely ignoring or misunderstanding this remark. "What about me?—I have to look at it every night. Sometimes it drives me mad." J. stared at him frostily enough, but must have decided it would be pointless to continue.

In the night I woke up hearing low voices coming from the compound parking lot, with the sound of wheels on gravel. I went to the window. There was no moon, and in the absolute blackness I could not see and so went back to sleep. In the morning we made ready to leave. A young boy carried out suitcases, and J. had gone into the lobby to pay the bill. As I wandered out into the driveway, I noticed that a truck which had stood by the flowerbeds behind the garages last night was now parked in a slightly different place, and something lay in the back, covered by a tarp. My heart contracted with fear to see this ominous shape, the size of a large animal. It was just the size of a lion or a cheetah, could even be a zebra. I walked closer, pretending, in case anyone saw me, to be looking at a bird that rustled in the hedge.

The manner in which the thing was covered made it obvious that it was contraband. I steeled myself against the sight of the glassy dead eyes of a lion, or some other creature I had so recently admired in life. Or a cache of ivory, perhaps. When I thought the porter was looking the other way, I reached out and lifted the corner of the tarpaulin. Underneath was the tree orchid, pried off its support during the night. Were they going to sell it? Transplant it here? I was both relieved that it wasn't a dead animal and indignant that some other living thing had been despoiled.

I was overcome, however, by irresistible desire. I could, by reaching out my hand, break off two rhizomes, enough to propagate. Of course I wouldn't do it—you'd have to smuggle it into the United States, for one thing. "No plant material," said the signs in Customs. I hesitated. I remembered a time when, unable to finish the lobster served on a flight from Cancun, I had wrapped it in my napkin and put it in the carry-on, thinking we would eat it for supper. Then J., with the carry-on, had been apprehended by customs officers and dragged away as censoriously as they might have dragged the most desperate drug smuggler.

When I realized that J. had seen me looking at the flowers, I knew he would be thinking of that. On the other hand, the memory of the bright blossoms filled me with covetousness. Two little segments would never be noticed in my purse, rescued from the evil White Hunter's despicable and illegal designs.

Armed with this defiant, self-justifying argument, I detached the two segments and put them in my purse, and went back to the washroom in the lobby to moisten some tissue to fold around the broken ends.

But I told myself this would be my last wicked act. If J. objected, I would explain that I knew I shouldn't do it, but that I was at the end of my rope about people. That was the feeling this place gave you. The feeling welled up, in the ladies' room, that people were hopeless. Widespread travel encourages deepest misanthropy. People kill each other and innocent creatures, they plunder the trees and burn the grasses. Who could countenance the savagery of their killing, the vulgarity of their lusts? The arrogance of the idea of hunting, the selfish brutality? The force of these emotions overcame me. I was tired of travel and wished to live a simple life among flowers—stolen orchids—and animals. A woman cannot do much, but I could become a friend of the sad dogs owned by feeble old people I saw in the streets, being dragged along on leashes, underfed. I would befriend cats, like a mad old cat lady, and grow orchids and African violets and live to myself.

The tree orchid did live for a time on a piece of bark in my kitchen. How I nourished it, consulted books, fed, watered, withheld water, misted, and cherished it. It put out a little root, but then a brown rot began to consume its leaves, and, over a week, ate them away.

Fellow Travelers

Chaque homme porte en lui sa dose d'opium naturel.
                              CHARLES BAUDELAIRE

I was taking the Air France flight from Paris to Hong Kong,
with a refueling stop in Moscow, planning to meet J. in the
transit lounge of the Hong Kong airport and fly with him
to Taipei for the wedding of one of our children, Colin.

J. and I have seven children. Four of them—one could
say *most* of them—live in other lands than America. If I were
a professional mother, I would always be on planes.

On the flight to Hong Kong, my mind was full of the
wedding I had just come from, of our youngest daughter,
Fannie, full of the agitating emotions that weddings produce,
and of reflections about how strange it was that our children,
from families of absolute ethnic monotony during a century
or two, should now spin off to the ends of the earth with
people of other races, creeds, and nations. On the whole I
like it, but I think it must mean something, too. I myself
had never been east of the Mississippi River until I was
twenty.

J. had been unable to attend Fannie's wedding because he
was deep in China, up north by the North Korean border.
On the plane I tried to read a paperback thriller that seemed
to describe what was perhaps befalling J. even as I read. It
was the story of an American doctor, teaching at Peking
Union Medical College, exactly as J. had been doing. The
doctor in the book was watched closely by his Chinese hosts,

suspected of being a spy, and was involuntarily drawn into intrigue and danger. Now J. had gone up into the northern provinces around Shenyang, and I had disloyally gone to the wedding instead. Perhaps he would be drawn into intrigue and danger. The doctor in the book made love to a beautiful Chinese woman, also a doctor, who planned to defect with him.

I had trouble reading because I was still feeling rather tearful, moved by Fannie's wedding in Paris, and the prospect of Colin's, and by the oddness of our children marrying in remote places outside America. Other people's children were doing this too, and one had to ask why? Or why not?

Perhaps Fannie's wedding had been unusually trying; I felt tearful and shaken. I often visit my children, and then flee from them, throw myself on planes sniffling tearfully, gripped by paroxysms of maternal remorse. I had left Paris in exactly this state the last time I visited Fannie, when she was a student at the Sorbonne, and had seemed so young and damageable. Come to think of it, I tend to feel tearful on planes as I do at the opera—there's something about the neutral solitude, and the feeling of being in mortal peril, suspended outside the world, that introduces some dramatic process of catharsis.

Of our seven children, one lives in Japan and another lives in Washington, D.C.—inside the beltway, as they say, which might as well be Japan, it's nearly as far for us, and with customs as foreign. Another lives in Hawaii, and the ones in Taipei and Paris.

Fannie's wedding in France: the ceremony had taken place at the *mairie*, a civil ceremony, and the wedding party was afterward at Benoît's (the groom's) brother's house. During the preparations, Fannie had pulled open a cupboard door

and cut her forehead. Blood trickled down her face. It hardly
seemed auspicious. And that in turn had reminded me of
another time she'd cut her forehead, and that in turn reminded me of the time she'd broken her leg, when she was
four, how tiny she had looked, lying there with her little
limb tangled in a wrong position. One has an endless stream
of traumatic maternal memories, and all of them were rushing
in on me now, it seemed, perhaps a consequence of airplane
travel. The plane crashes and I never get to tell them of my
love, or where I've hidden my jewelry.

This wedding party had been concocted by Fannie and
Benoît themselves, and Benoît's brothers. They had refused
to let the mothers help, I suspect to avoid any dissension
between Benoît's parents, who are divorced—somewhat unusual for French people, though divorce, they say, is catching
on in France. The father, Henri, is a Catholic; Dominique,
the mother, is a Protestant; one is right-wing, one left-wing;
and so on. These social divisions precluded any sort of church
ceremony for Fannie and Benoît, and kept the young couple
from accepting help from either parent for fear of seeming
to favor the *culte* of one over the other.

So the reception was held at the house of Benoît's brother
Bernard, which turned out to be a sort of potting shed behind
another house in a working-class suburb. It was furnished in
what one might call international graduate student—white
Formica table, bookshelves of boards and cement blocks,
lots of stereo equipment. A chic touch out of fashionable
films—the old Citroën car seats as chairs, made of expensive
real leather. Into this little house would crowd the dozens of
French relatives, solid bourgeois both Protestant and Catholic, stout aunts and distant cousins and college friends, kids
from Benoît's lycée and his *grande école*. Fannie didn't know
any of them, of course. They had rented a dozen white tables

and dozens of chairs for the garden; therefore it rained horrendously, volumes of unstinting French rain in great sheets on the floundering late tulips.

To the misery and metaphorical ominousness of the downpour was added another source of tension, which Fannie confided to me as a dangerous moment drew near: it was that Benoît's mother and father had not spoken to each other— had not even seen each other—since their rancorous divorce. Nor had their two families seen each other—these two families who would now be confined together in the potting shed out of the steamy rain.

And not only that: Benoît and Fannie knew that the father, Henri, planned to bring along his girlfriend, Madame Roemy. He'd asked if he could, and Benoît, worried that otherwise his father might not come at all, had said of course, bring her. But then they'd decided not to tell Dominique, the mother, and now they were beginning to feel jittery about what would happen. Dominique looked very young and pretty, but perhaps Madame Roemy would be only thirty or even younger? How was Dominique going to feel? What would she do? I thought that at least they should have warned her.

Fannie and Benoît hadn't warned her because they were afraid she'd go home. They thought instead that if their parents just got the dreaded confrontation over with, then everything would be all right ever after.

"Ha, ha," I said.

How glad I was to be away from it and sitting in the cozy limbo of the plane. I think it was the longest day of my life. It's hard anyway to be absolutely jolly in a driving rain among dozens of French strangers, endlessly saying, "*Je suis la mère de Fannie*" to each new group that crowded into the impossibly cramped little house, answering their questions in my idiotic French—*"Oui, de Californie, oui, très contente."* I couldn't help feeling wistful, though I was rather ashamed of it, about the midwestern country club wedding receptions of my girlhood, the catered cakes and acres of petits fours, and the driveways full of Cadillacs and Buick convertibles.

I felt ashamed of myself for wishing, even if just for a minute, for all that bridelike business for Fannie, because J. and I had been rather derisive when his daughter Emma had had just such a wedding, in Southern California, where her mother lives—six or eight bridesmaids, rainbow tulle, matching coats for all the men, and, in contrast to the furtive and dreaded rencontre of the divorced parents in France, at Emma's wedding the divorced parents and stepparents—nine of us altogether—were obliged to line up holding bouquets and submit to group photos. There were so many combinations of divorced and remarried stepparents that one of the bridesmaids was married to her stepbrother. Very California, very America now.

As I sat on the plane thinking about my children and their weddings, a new woman moved herself into the vacant seat next to me, smiling apologetically. She indicated her old seat, across the aisle, where a young mother was putting her sleeping baby. The young mother included me in her smile of thanks. Airplane survival strategies, a hierarchy of needs and cooperation. When the new woman had glanced covertly at my book, ascertaining what language it was written in, she spoke. She was from New York—and I fell into conversation with her, breaking my most sacred rule for airplane travel: never talk to the person next to you. Her name was Marcia. She told me about her daughter, who lived in England with a British biochemist, and her son in Mali, who had married a Javanese.

"They sent red wedding invitations," she said.

"In China, the bride wears red. A color of luck and happiness," I said. "Why do you think they're all leaving? Middle-class American children living in Taiwanese walk-ups and Prague garrets?"

"They'll come back," the woman said. "After all, it's an American tradition—Paris, travel, adventure. Then they come home."

"I'm not so sure," I said. "They're enrolling their kids in Japanese nursery schools. They're learning Afghani." I began to run on a bit about how though we had all been taught to believe—by our parents, who did devoutly believe—that America was the most comfortable, safest, and best place to live, this was no longer true. The streets are dangerous, we are imprisoned in cars, gun-infested ugliness has settled over it all, and a mood of malice and suspicion. Our suburbs are hideous and our little third-world towns are a hell of junked cars and billboards.

Marcia looked dubious at this. "Just you try using an English washing machine and see how you like it. And have you seen their fridges the size of shoe boxes?"

"What does your daughter say?"

"Oh well, she's young, the young will put up with anything."

Of our children, Emma is the only one to have married someone like us—the rest have married exotically, to use the word in its anthropological sense. They have married people of other races, religions, and nations. Is this a criticism of us, or a compliment? For instance, Annie, the wife of our eldest son, Adam, is Hawaiian, Samoan, Japanese, and

Chinese, and was brought up in Hawaii, which is like a foreign land. Standing in the French rain at Fannie's wedding had reminded me of Hawaii, the same wet, vegetable odor, the heat, and the French potting shed had reminded me of Adam's house in Hawaii, insubstantial and shacklike. Our Hawaiian children live in a sort of compound with Annie's Japanese mother, and a tangle of succulents and strange tropical flowers, and piles of lumber in between the guest cottage, where they live, and the bigger house, where Annie's mother lives, and a jungle gym and lizards. But it was another day that Fannie's wedding made me think of. The actual day of Adam's wedding, the roast pig and poi and so on, must have been conflated in my mind with later, because the baby was already running around. Annie being that mixture of Japanese and Samoan and so on—of course their child is beautiful. But what does it matter? Adam and Annie have split up already, and Adam has taken up with an Australian with a punk haircut. Life on the Pacific Rim.

Now there's Colin, my most precariously situated child, living his strange life in Taiwan, teaching English and working in a trading company, whatever that is, and as usual looking for something else, without any idea how to go about finding it, and speaking in Mandarin. In tongues, it might as well be, it sounds so strange coming from this fair, blue-eyed person. We're delighted that he is at last going to marry his girlfriend Laura. She's pretty and sensible—an American, actually. I had expected he would marry a Chinese, which, of course, would also have been all right. Laura's mother is from Yugoslavia.

If anyone in my family, any relative or ancestor, had ever left the shores of America (save for the first arrivals, of course), I had never heard of it. Family lore did not congratulate travelers, except in the cases of our fathers, in the First War.

My father said that his first sight of Venice had been the most thrilling moment of his life, and that if I were ever in Milan I must eat at Savini. And so I have, and stayed at the Danielli, where he stayed, and the rest. He would have liked to have been a traveler, I think. But he was not, no more than the rest of them, going to DAR meetings in their print dresses and (paradoxical) Eleanor Roosevelt hats, in their Packard cars. They had no imaginative contact whatever with Europe or anywhere else—England, perhaps, excepted, the testimony of the matched sets of Dickens and Thackeray in their attics.

When I first visited Colin in Taiwan, I thought Taiwan was the worst place in the world, so crowded and chaotic, so full of neon and rain and strange cuttlefish dishes, and little sacks of garbage deposited at the foot of every staircase. Clearly Colin and Laura like their life there. They drink tea, and have furniture with dragons carved on it. They go to the weddings of Chinese friends, and pay visits to the families of their students—Laura's a teacher too—and walk in the busy night streets, eating boiled fish bought from street vendors. But on my first visit, the traffic, the difficulty in changing a plane reservation, the rain, and the inevitable quarrel with Colin got me down. I just couldn't get out fast enough. All I could think of was getting to Paris.

Seven children. They marry, and next babies come along, and then the number at home at Christmas begins to be enormous—nineteen last Christmas. I exchanged some of this information with Marcia. She told me about her recent visit to London. I began to tell her about Fannie's wedding.

In the Paris potting shed: another of my daughters, Deb, was there, and her new husband, Andy. They had been married in Maryland a few weeks before. We weren't at that wedding, but that's another story. Andy is part Jewish, raised a Catholic, and is a Republican, which makes him as exotic as any of the other people our children have brought home. His father works for the CIA. I love these exotic new family members, all of them, they give a spin to things. They lend to our children, so familiar to us already, the unexpected polish of mystery.

In the French potting shed, Deb and Andy were helping me unwrap the tarts. Uncles arrived, cases of wine, cases of champagne arrived, a giant block of pâté, a wheel of Brie. Aunt Micheline brought bread from Strasbourg, and a wooden salver the size of a tire to put it on.

Cousins and school friends arrived, in strange getups of black leather, or denim, with the little round glasses, yellow fingers, and bitten nails of French students, smoking incessantly. They were rather frightening looking, but when you talked to them they were all polite bourgeois children, with their perfect English and nice French manners. They helped me set out the paper plates and plastic cups.

I have to admit the paper plates deepened my misery. I couldn't help but feel they were having paper plates and plastic cups because we were Americans. I believed that all French believe that all Americans believe that it's okay to have plastic cups. They think we always eat on paper plates. A French lady living in San Francisco shocked us all once by serving the first course at her elegant dinner party on paper plates, in apparent confidence that she was doing the straightforward California thing. The possibilities of cultural misunderstanding are so vast! It made me wonder how many we were perpetuating right there at Fannie's wedding party. Had we failed to bring something the mother of the bride ought always to bring? Dragées? Something baked? "*Merci, Madame,*" the students all said when I handed out food, as if I had prepared it. The father, Henri, didn't come and didn't come.

The stewardess came by and we ordered vodkas, Marcia and I both. Only now, settling in with our drinks, did I really look at her. She had the fidgety look of deep unease some people on planes have, and tore at her cocktail napkin with her long red nails.

My disappointment with Fanny's reception, and my fears of cultural misunderstanding, had also put me in mind of the wedding of Brent—our second son—to Jilleen, an Irish girl. Jilleen's mother then had been disappointed just the way I was disappointed in Paris. It was the first wedding of any of her daughters, and was taking place in far-off America. The reception was held at a family beach cottage, very very funky, and I remember seeing her face—disappointment, if not shock. There was no way one could explain to them the value of this real estate—it just looked to them like a shabby, flea-ridden little hippie shack on the beach.

Now *that* was a stressful wedding. To the mysteriousness of alien cultures were added the mysteries of Catholicism and a false priest. Jilleen, who always said she was not religious, had been seized, as the wedding day grew nearer, with the wish to be married in the Church. For the sake of her parents, she said. They're called Maureen and William. Maureen and William were coming from Dublin for the wedding, as were Jilleen's three sisters, Uncle Piers and Aunt Bridgit, the husbands of the three sisters, and someone else I've forgotten. The details had unfolded over the course of several weeks, in a series of shocks.

Of course we had said we would be happy to put up Jilleen's relatives, not realizing there would be eleven of them and they'd be staying a month. Then one day I happened to ask

Brent if he was taking Catholic instruction, which I'd always heard was necessary if a Protestant married a Catholic even if you didn't intend to convert (which of course would have horrified us). We thought of our own mothers and of their midwestern horror of Catholics. Our mothers were terrified we would ruin our health by being denied birth control and forced to bear families of ten and twelve. Since in the town where I grew up there were no blacks or Jews or any other recognizable ethnic minority, Catholic was as alluringly Other as you could get.

Brent explained that he didn't have to take instruction because they had found a truly reasonable priest who didn't believe in it—a colorful, beloved figure around San Francisco, who was even a bishop, one who thought all those rules were bullshit, it was enough to be a sincere, good person.

That didn't sound right even to me, who knew nothing about Catholicism really. I asked a Catholic friend to whom it didn't sound right either, and she did the straightforward thing of calling and asked at the diocese. They said, "Oh, no, is that crazy old guy up to his tricks again?" Of course he wasn't a priest at all, but a madman.

This was only a week before the wedding, with the invitations sent out, the church booked, the parents literally on their plane. J. and I were faced with a delicate decision: should we tell Brent his priest was an imposter and let him decide how to tell, or whether to tell, Jilleen? Or should we say nothing and let the thing go ahead as planned? I suppose if we had believed in priests, or in these ceremonies, and considered them binding in heaven, we would not even have considered concealing what we knew. But to us one form of make-believe seemed much like another. If you think you are married, aren't you married? To get a real priest now, who would insist on the rules, would have meant the incal-

culable nuisance of postponing the wedding. But of course
we did finally tell Brent, who made the decision that Jilleen
must be told.

Jilleen was monumentally distraught and went to bed at
midday with cloths over her forehead, like someone in a
movie, moaning with self-reproach. Her parents were on their
way; her mother would instantly sense the inauthenticity of
the priest; she, Jilleen, should have sensed it, but what had
she known of the American clergy? Above all, what was to
be done?

J. and I had moved out of our house. At the prospect of
eleven houseguests, J. had hit on the idea of inventing an
imaginary business trip, and, maintaining the fiction of our
absence, we had just handed our place over to the Irish family.
We were to get home the day of the rehearsal dinner, and
they were to make themselves absolutely at home in the
meantime. In fact we had borrowed a friend's apartment.
Our children have always complained about our lack of so-
ciability, so we felt a little guilty about this latest defection;
but we did it nonetheless, and thus were officially absent,
not in a position to be much help with the new crisis even
if we'd known what to do.

The O'Brians arrived, installed themselves in our house,
and immediately took charge of the false priest emergency.
It was anticlimactic in that there was no problem. After many
transatlantic phone calls and cables, a dispensation was ob-
tained from Rome, a new priest was found, and the wedding
was saved. A lifetime of piety had paid off.

A few days before the wedding, I discovered I had forgotten
something vital at home, so I had to abandon the fiction of
being away. I rang to say I was back early and could I pop
in for some things? When I got there, they were all at dinner.
It was odd to find a group of strangers at my dinner table,

with the good dishes and glasses out, a roast of beef, delicious smells. "Ah, you must be Dinny," they said, infinitely hospitable. "Come in, dear. Sit you right down here, there's a love, and take a little meat." In the kitchen I saw they had laid in a huge sack of potatoes.

If the O'Brians were reassured by our comfortable house that Brent's family was at least solvent, the beach house gave them pause. Like my memory of midwestern weddings, with their centerpieces as large as altarpieces and their cakes the size of ponies, Jilleen's mother had, I could see, a memory or a dream of her beautiful daughter marrying wealth, but, more than that, elegance. Perhaps she had dreamed of a huge church wedding, a white satin dress with a train, aristocratic guests. Instead, here were a bunch of laid-back, hairy cousins passing a joint around out on the beach, with balloons and rock music. The Californian equivalent of the Parisian potting shed. I didn't blame her for being upset.

These thoughts had helped me forget the basically unnatural state in which we found ourselves. For the traveler, time is suspended in an airplane as in a space capsule; one neither ages nor remembers. Life will start again on arrival. The brain slows cryonically; if you are one of those travelers who must drink or take a pill to be able to bear it at all (I am), you are often quite literally drugged. I relaxed. I continued my stories of weddings.

Almost as if to mock my stuporous lethargy, the plane now gave a tremendous shudder and began to drop like a stone for several seconds; people screamed slightly late, our stomachs sickened, trays and glasses smashed. Then it seemed to right itself and resume its forward motion through the sky. Marcia, next to me, clasped me as if I were a child to be protected. She released me. "Dear God," she said. Someone began to cry. I thought of J. Marcia leaned back and closed her eyes.

In seconds, the voice of the pilot, in the cowboy drawl that even French pilots seem to employ, came on to say something about turbulence, downdraft, and calm. We sat back in our seats, strapped ourselves more closely in, our blood humming, relishing the relief of still being alive, still suspended, droning through the night. Now it was as if our attention to flying was needed in order to hold the airplane up; our collective will at work, mine as passionately as Marcia's, or the young mother's, or that of the stewardess who walked up and down the aisle, checking the seat belts. The worst had not happened.

Fear blotted out the interest in things. I had a mind only for thoughts of airplane disasters, resolutions to become a better person, mental apologies to the children and J. I should have gone to China with J., I thought. How could I express pious affirmations of family life when I was running away, was not at his side, had begun to pick and choose among places and privations, refusing some? Guiltily returning to my paperback book, I could not but think that it would serve me right if J. met the beautiful Chinese doctor. "Are you going to have another vodka?" I asked Marcia.

"Yeah, I think I will." She sighed.

She told me about her son's Javanese wedding. "It sounds lovely," I said. "All weddings are lovely, don't you think? Even if you think they will end badly and that the couple aren't suited. Of course I never let myself think that."

The pilot spoke again. "*Mesdames et messieurs*, we are going to have to land at Leningrad. It is for inspection of a mechanical malfunction. We do not expect to be on the ground for long." No further explanation. Almost at once, the plane began to descend.

"Leningrad?"

"I don't care where, I'll be glad to be on the ground," Marcia said.

We landed. Nothing about the airport except the lettering on the trucks that attended the landing could have suggested Russia. We disembarked to wait in the departure lounge. Here things were more specifically Russian—Stolichnaya and nesting wooden dolls for sale in the Beriozka shop at one end of the shabby little lobby. People paced around, bought Pepsi from the drinks counter, sat in piles of carryons and coats, grumbling. A wait of an hour became two, then three, with no word forthcoming from Air France, or from Russia, about our situation.

Marcia and I were now a pair, watched each other's bags, made desultory talk, shopped. I bought a half dozen amber necklaces for people for Christmas. "I can get you some Gorby dolls," the salesgirl whispered.

Waiting is an important downside of travel, I thought. If you can't wait, making your mind a blank, read posters, and watch people, you can't travel. It was four hours before an Air France man told us that the plane would not be leaving until the next day, and that we would be taken to a hotel. It was necessary that we stay together, he emphasized. We could not leave the hotel, and we had to submit our passports now; those not wishing to surrender their passports could remain in the transit lounge.

This seemed a welcome development. The blood of the traveler quickens a little to think of new sights, welcomes unexpected adventures. I had never been to Russia. A sigh of exigencies rose up from the passengers, even as they formed an untidy queue to hand over their travel documents, most preferring the unknown to the known. Some were unhappy, pressed, needed to get to Hong Kong, were missed, were missing something.

We were to be conveyed in parties of five in taxis, battered cars that looked like old Chryslers from my childhood. The stout, impassive drivers leaned against their fenders scrutinizing us and jockeying for the passengers who looked most promising. Marcia and I, the woman with the baby, and a young American man, black, got in one. To judge from the disgusted and mistrustful expression of the driver, he thought himself unlucky to have drawn us. He had a large, Mussulman mustache and deep Boris Godunov voice.

"Marlboros?" he asked. Health-conscious Americans and new mothers did not of course smoke. We apologized. The young man, who told us his name was Arlen, had some Luckies, and offered the driver a pack.

"No Marlboros?"

"Sorry," Arlen said. The driver accepted the Luckies.

Once on the road from the airport, this taciturn individual began to tell us his story, perhaps for the pleasure of telling it, perhaps because he liked us. He had a resigned, defeated air that seemed not to expect anything from us once the possibility of Marlboros had been laid to rest. He wished us to know he was not a taxi driver but a literary critic. Not even a failed literary critic, a successful one. His name was Yuri. He had often been to Paris and Berlin and New York; we must not think him an average Russian with no ideas beyond the Don River. He drove the taxi because his girlfriend was so angry with him she would not marry him. Why was she angry? What had she to be angry about? She who would have a new, fine apartment, earned by his accomplishments as a famous literary critic, his reward for fame and service? Because there was no furniture. What good is a new apartment without furniture? How can you have your friends in, how live? To have a grand apartment and no furniture was almost worse than to have stayed in the old place with its miserable sticks. There one was surrounded by the familiar, and was not the object of the envy and conniving of others. On the other hand, a grand, empty apartment was somehow culpable and arriviste. Yet to get some furniture would require six months of his time. He would have to give up his writing and his magazine and all his other literary activities.

"Why is that?" we asked, obliging him with our questions.

He smiled his rather vulpine smile. "I believe you call it networking. I estimate it would take me six months of networking because, you see, what does a literary critic have that others want? The answer is: nothing. I start from negative. I used to cover the PEN Congress in East Berlin. From there you could sometimes bring back something—a book or a film with naked women in it, brought from West Berlin. This would give you something to bargain with. But my term is expired to the PEN Congress. Also, with perestroika, nude films and that sort of thing is not a novelty."

"Look what the girl at the Beriozka got me," said Marcia, opening her purse. She carefully unscrewed the wooden doll painted to look like Gorbachev. Inside him was Brezhnev, and inside him Khrushchev, and inside him Stalin, and inside him, Lenin. "They are forbidden, the girl told me. I got three sets," said Marcia, "one for each of my married daughters. She gave them to me in the ladies' room. She was taking a big risk."

It was our good luck that the hotel was on the other side of Leningrad from the airport, giving us a look at the beautiful streets of the old city of St. Petersburg. Here and there women stood in the infamous lines in front of stores with windows painted over. It was now dusk, and lights went on indoors, giving glimpses of interiors—bare rooms lit by beautiful chandeliers reflected in French-looking mirrors, splendor that shabbiness barely dimmed. The palaces were red or turquoise, the onion domes shone like illustrations in a children's book. The taxi crossed the river, heading toward the harbor. In the street, as we came into the suburbs, a knot of women sat with tomatoes spread out before them. The hotel was an imposing modern hotel, the Baltiskaya, built by Finns. Inside, it could have been any international luxury hotel of marble and brass. The rooms looked out on the Baltic. It was an unexpected ending to the day.

I washed, and set out the few items I kept in my carryon. I had begun this morning in France, if it was still today and not some other day. The long hours, the changing light, had blurred the distinction of night and morning. In China it would be night. J. would still be in Shenyang, eating sea slugs or beetles. A goose flew alone over the gray Baltic water. I was in Russia, but not in Russia, couldn't see the Hermitage or the Summer Palace, was in hotel limbo. A sense of the deep, deep peace and comfort of hotel limbo came over me.

Marcia tapped at my hotel room door, face anxious. "Oh, God, we'll never get out of here," she wailed. "I should have stayed in California, I knew it."

"Think of it as a free trip to Russia. Anyway, nothing bad can happen in a first-class hotel." I laughed.

"Giardiasis. They have terrible giardiasis in Russia. A friend of mine got it and had it for a year. They couldn't cure it. Whatever you do, don't drink this water."

"This is bottled water."

"Not even the bottled water. This is Leningrad. Maybe

the water is all right in Moscow, but not here. Everybody tells you that. Did you get through?"

"Get through?"

"The phone. All I got was 'Nyet, nyet.' Does anyone know we're here? I tried to call home, but nyet."

I was surprised, for Marcia had seemed so sanguine about travel, but I quickly recognized these querulous tones: traveler's panic. Thrown by the unexpected into a feeling that you will never see again the beloved, never sleep in your own bed. I'd had this feeling lots of times, but not now.

No one had said we couldn't prowl in the hotel. I went down to the lobby to look for the bar, never doubting I would find one. Sometimes the strangeness of the world delights, but sometimes the sameness oppresses. There is always a bar. No doubt the protection and cover of a first-class hotel are indispensable for a woman traveling alone, but you can't help but regret the sameness, regret that things are denied to women traveling alone—the romance of seedy bars in port cities, talking to sailors, hearing the adventures of real adventurers, risk-taking mercenaries, and killers. Maybe when you got to be an old woman these things opened up. As it was, your interest was bound to be misunderstood. Once I leaned against a wall, in Paris, because my high-heeled shoes hurt. "Here, here, move along," a gendarme told me, and his expression showed what he thought I was. No doubt there were women higher-spirited than I, or harder up for excitement, who would brave the hot tropical nights to meet sailors. I admire women reporters, especially the ones who go to war, and battlefield nurses. Maybe I would pick up a Russian, just for drinks, to hear his story here safely under the cover of Air France and the Baltiskaya. I recognized the warming of my blood to the idea of adventure, even if overseen by Intourist.

The halls were further evidence that in Russia, in China, in Cincinnati, good hotels are always the same—though in Xi'an once, we had been in a hotel of a splendor unimaginable in Cincinnati, and distinguished from any other in the world (I suppose) by a river that ran down the middle of the immense lobby. On one side of the river, delicious Chinese food was served by waitresses in lovely cheongsams for Chinese diners, or private travelers like ourselves, and, on the other, a lavish buffet of imitation Western food was spread for the groups of Canadian tourists brought through on buses, Chinese and Western diners to stare at each other over the gulf of water, the twain never to meet. The Canadian tourists as they speared butter pats and radishes from beds of crushed ice and were made to eat mashed potatoes and meatballs from a chafing dish, as in Toronto, darting hostile glances across this separating stream at the gourmandizing Chinese dignitaries.

In the elevator of this Russian hotel, certain cultural differences reasserted themselves. Instead of "instructions" for operating the elevator, there were "rules" for its use, and these were expressed in terms of what was forbidden. "It is forbidden to more than four persons. It is forbidden to exit between floors."

Once in a Japanese hotel, when I threw away some photographs of us with a princess of Japan who had been the patron of J.'s meeting, these photos were rescued somewhere deep in the bottom of the hotel, by someone who knew which room they had come from, and returned to us by the management, with a tactful bow. People watch you in first-class hotels. It is forbidden to throw away pictures of the princess.

In the bar everyone was excited. The other Air France passengers crowded in, ordering champagne on credit cards. I sat with Marcia and Arlen, we three Americans. With our plastic, we were rich, but so were the locals who flocked in here to spend their hard currency. All were by local standards rich, rich, rich, and they were celebrating. The band had an accordion and violins. You expected the Hopek, you expected a bear on a chain. A raft of Irish girls danced with portly Russians in blouses, seeming to celebrate escape from Ireland and their priests and mothers. A bride, with a headdress that stood out over her ears like the wings of a dragonfly, danced with an old man in an embroidered jacket.

"It's really not so bad here," Arlen said. "I was in Moscow, and it wasn't so bad there either. They have leather bars. There are lots of painters. Theater. I went out with some waiters when they got off work. The whole time was spent arguing with cabdrivers about the prices of rides, but it was sort of sweet."

"I hope you didn't drink the water in Moscow, dear," Marcia said.

It was true: here were people being happy in Russia. Our own children are not so trapped in the pieties that our parents believed in and tried to tell us. That we were more free, for example, that America had invented freedom. Recently I read something that said six countries, objectively considered, are more "free" than we. Plenty of countries are more prosperous than we. When I first realized that—when I saw the gleaming trains of Europe and Gothic cathedrals recently polished, and the oyster stands beneath umbrellas outside restaurants, and entire families with their skis for their *vacances d'hiver*, even the warm bread smells floating out at every corner, and the chic dogs, while back home people live in shabby, dispirited suburbs, and there are no trains to speak of, only the desperate cabdrivers in their dented heaps conniving with one another as if it were Istanbul: New York, with the blight of Queens and the Bronx like burning rubble on the way in from the airport—when I first saw all this I felt betrayed. People had been lying. Ours was not the land of dreams, nor theirs the lands of hungry, huddled masses, not anymore.

I suppose our parents had been thinking of war-torn Europe. They had seen the newsreels, or had been there in the First War, and had since lost track. Could not believe that we had become shabby, dangerous, and ugly, like much of the third world, while Europe had reclaimed its grandeur, its comfort, its elegance and joie de vivre. We had lost perspective and clung to our self-satisfaction. No wonder the children had split. Our children had not been fed that particular propaganda, and saw things as they found them: comfort there, problems here. Why stay here?

"I think I've scored some caviar," said Marcia, whose earlier panic had now been replaced by the expression of wily satisfaction seen on all tourist shoppers. "He's going to bring it to the room at midnight. That waiter there. Thirteen dollars for two hundred fifty-gram jars. Are you going to get some?" The open matron now had the calculation of a dealer, the pride of an entrepreneur. American know-how.

"Sure," I said.

"Sure," said Arlen.

Poor J. in uncomfortable Shenyang, or perhaps he was by now in Hong Kong. Any worries about him seemed far away, that effect of travel by which real life is left behind, and a new reality, the here and now, is more important. The new difficulties of the here and now make the old seem flat and simple. I felt an intense pleasure merely in being, here, this minute. The absence of the normal context proves that you exist independent of it, you, a being, alive. Here I am, a woman alone in the Soviet Union, and I will go on being me. The world is interesting and the food not bad (as long as you pay in hard currency). Thinking like this, I was filled

with the happiest of traveler's emotions, an existential sense
of belonging—of belonging, moreover, against great odds,
of being proven and seasoned, of knowing about visas and
menus in lots of languages, possessed of several functioning
credit cards, a reassuring supply of sleeping pills, aspirin,
and anticystitis medicine, a Swiss army knife, enough soap.
Better than all this, the sense of contentment merely to be,
a complete human unit who could continue in this new or
some other place were all the rest of the world to drop away,
and you to remain in the hard-currency bar of an international
hotel in Russia.

"You didn't tell me what happened to Henri and Dominique,
the parents of your son-in-law. Was that their names?" Marcia
asked.

  "Henri came with his mistress, Madame Roemy, and Dominique rose to the occasion with gracious smiles. There was
only one awkward moment, when Dominique said to the
mistress, 'I think we have already met, Madame. *On se connaît
déjà.*' Once in Geneva, at—whatever it was. Obviously she
had mixed her up with some other woman she'd caught Henri
with. Madame Roemy said, 'No, you are mistaken: *Vous vous
êtes trompée, Madame,*' which sounds such a devastating put-
down, though I think it's just polite French."

  "Was she pretty—the new girlfriend?"

  "Not nearly as pretty as Dominique, which was a great
relief to everybody. She had on a terrific dress, though."

  Marcia laughed. Arlen lit one of his Luckies. My two best
friends. What need of family, or familiar things? We watched
the elderly Finns, ebulliently drunk, do old-fashioned jit-
terbugging to the high-school dance music. We watched the
Russian musicians in their cowboy hats. Watched platters of

acceptable-looking cabbage piroshki going by. At a table to my left sat two beautiful, sulking British tarts, who quarreled with their good-looking Russian gangster boyfriends. I had never been here before and yet I thought I understood it all, and it all filled me with love, and I was in no hurry at all to get to Hong Kong.

In the Land of
the Patriarchs

How I came into it hardly matters—I had met the Hetter family some months before, when I had come to Utah with a film director, Volker Schlondorff, who planned to make a movie about the death of a Mormon martyr, Rawsell Hetter, and about his wife Reba and the six children, living on for his memory. Rawsell Hetter had been murdered ten years before by the Utah authorities after a standoff that began when he refused to send his children to school. Volker and I had arrived in Utah as travelers for whom the Hetters were natives as exotic as Amazonian tribes, and we, to them, were city dwellers, and suspect.

Before we went to Utah, Volker had sent me a tape taken off local television news at the time of the killing of Rawsell Hetter. It was like a travelogue showing the first events in the strange sequence; there was the delightful Wasatch range, Tibetan in its loftiness, the charming sheep that grazed the lower slope, the dramatic blue-purple of the sky. The little red schoolhouse was purely American, with the attractive parents and six sturdy children ranged in front of it, all dressed in frontier clothes, as if costumed for "Little House on the Prairie." The mother and little girls wore lace caps, the father and boys were in jeans and plaid flannel shirts. They were all blonds or redheads, the littlest boys with hair of brightest gold, and even the mother's was an undarkened halo. They shone with righteousness. This was the Hetter family, whose lives now had darkened. In the tape they were smiling trustfully for the camera, not seeing what lay before them: that the polygamous father would take a plural wife, and that he would die. If photographs of vanished people are sad, videos even more poignantly remind of transience and vanished happiness.

Volker and I stayed in Park City and drove into the countryside looking for the Hetter place. Park City, Utah, a ski resort in winter, in summer and fall becomes a ghost town given over to small conventions and meetings, of groups of policymakers or legislators, a film festival, a writers' conference. Ten miles from Park City, all the ambiance of prosperity and comfort disappears, and the traveler finds himself in the stony foothills of the Wasatch, with their scraggly pastures, flocks of sheep, and poor little towns, each with its diner, its store selling motorcycles, small tractors, and snowmobiles, the Mormon church, a few modern bungalows, the trailer homes on the edge of town, and a few nineteenth-century houses, many with two or more entrances, one for each of the wives of some old Mormon patriarch. The lanes are strewn with miscellaneous auto parts and rusted farm implements, blighting landscapes of otherwise uplifting beauty, the blazing canary and crimson beech and poplar trees a legendary sight, everyone had assured us, in itself worth driving out into the countryside to see. A tourist attraction.

When Volker and I came to interview Reba Hetter, Rawsell had been dead for ten years, and the older children were grown. The Hetter children all looked alike: Ted, partly paralyzed from an accident, who worked at the garage, two younger boys, April, Rowena, and another sister, Margot— the lucky one who got away from home. We met red-haired

April, a tall, solemn, and beautiful young woman; the younger sister, flaxen-haired Rowena, heavily pregnant, with a querulous, pink-eyed look. These young women were now surrounded by a pack of undifferentiated little blond children of their own, and their own younger brothers. The young mothers treated them kindly but had an abstracted and detached way with them, as if too many had come along too quickly to allow them to learn their names or to take an interest in the way one might differ from another. With the husbands of Rowena and April, and the unborn baby in Rowena's belly, I counted the household at fourteen. The plural wife had long since taken off.

As we talked with the daughters, Reba Hetter herself came in. At a distance, she might have been April except for a difference in the hair color; the mother's was lighter, done up in a corona of braid on the top of her head. She was a woman of not yet forty, wearing a sweater and skirt, boots, and a denim jacket. She walked with a rapid, athletic stride, and was followed closely by a darkly handsome young man in jeans and a checked shirt who glared at us under his dark brows and disappeared into the kitchen. We took him to be one of her sons-in-law. Reba smiled at us. Until then she had seemed a beautiful woman. What was shocking was that she had no teeth.

This was the image that stayed in my mind—the affront and mystery of her toothlessness. No explanation sufficed to account for it—not poverty, for there were toys and a television set, appliances. An obsessive dread of dentists? A temporary thing, lost or broken dental plates, or teeth knocked out by some accident? I found it upsetting, an index of the poor woman's spiritual condition, she who had seen her husband shot before her eyes. For some time after our visit, Reba Hetter's face floated into a troubled dream—a strong, beautiful face, and then the mockery of beauty, her toothless smile. I had a sense of the meaning of this but could not find it. Perhaps it was Reba Hetter's act of protest. Whereas dentures and false teeth would be the symbols of servility, age, and defeat, this was defiance; it was as if to say, You have killed my husband before my eyes and made me helpless. An animal without teeth dies, but I am still here. Volker didn't find it as upsetting as I did; he found it ugly.

On the telephone that evening I told J. about Reba's teeth, but he related her condition prosaically to a lack of access to general health care. J.'s tone, concerned and doctorly, but also dispassionate and objective, was the same when he talked about Utah as about remote tribes of central Africa.

"Some of these people live in extremely primitive conditions," he said. "Especially the Indians, but many whites, too. In part it's poor access to health care, in part low awareness of hygiene." I said nothing. It had to mean more than that.

Reba Hetter was pleased that Volker thought of making a film of Rawsell's life; it would vindicate her husband. "I won't deny I could use the money, too," she said. "As you see, there are a lot of mouths to feed. I guess you want to hear all about it. Oh, I can talk about it. It's been ten years." Her voice was high, sincere, with that quavery intermountain accent of Utah and Colorado. "But I still feel I haven't made people feel, really feel, that moment when we saw our daddy fall."

Rawsell Hetter's death was the culmination, as Reba saw it, of a whole history of persecutions of the Hetter family, ending when the sheriff's men shot him with the whole family looking on. Before our visit to Utah, Volker and I had read all the newspaper accounts, and later we talked to Frank Murphy, the local librarian, who was writing a book on the case. We had a photo of the young Reba Hetter, then Reba Anderson, who had been an all-American girl in high school, a cheerleader with long blonde hair, like Rowena's now. There were photos of her in her white cowboy boots and pleated cheerleading skirt, modestly knee-length, reflecting both the fifties and the values of the Mormon community. She had been planning to go to Brigham Young University, but, in the summer between high school and college, she fell in love with Rawsell Hetter, a newcomer to town. Her parents had tried to stop Rawsell and Reba getting married; they didn't think he was good enough—objections predictable from parents of an only, beautiful daughter. Reba insisted that nobody understood Rawsell. She believed he was the gentlest and wisest person she'd ever met, and she believed he had an intuitive gift for understanding nature. This may have been true; for a while after the marriage he sold herbal remedies of his own concoction, and people who took one for a complaint said that they helped.

Rawsell was an orphan from Switzerland who had come to Lopex because he had an uncle there. From his photos it seems he was nice-looking, of medium height with a stocky, weathered build, like a frontiersman. People who knew Reba hinted that physical passion had caught her unaware, had seized her like an addiction. I thought, meeting her, that she may have liked being the center of a storm.

After their elopement they made their living in a variety of ways—he fixed television sets and tractor engines, and farmed a few acres that had been his uncle's. Reba put up jam and worked in the New Zion Diner. At first her mother would hardly speak to her, but little by little she came round to feeling that Rawsell, despite his foreign upbringing and accented speech, was at least a loyal, faithful husband and sincerely religious. Reba for her part never really forgave her mother for opposing their love. "It doesn't matter what people think, my sweet," Rawsell told her—that defiant stance of lovers through the ages—and it didn't, at first.

Then the babies began to arrive, rapidly, all born at home. The overburdened Reba rarely left the place, which they had enlarged, except to go to church regularly. Most people thought they were a lovely family at that period, the kids all so pretty and well-behaved, and Reba sewed their clothes, and the children did well in school. Volker and I were moved, anyone would be, at her account of their struggle, and of their love.

It was at church that things began to go wrong. Rawsell was a convert, no one knew from what, with a convert's way of taking things literally, or differently. He had fundamentalist leanings early on. It got so he would argue every Sunday about the text the others were studying. Mormons have discussions, taking a certain text every Sunday; the church chooses the texts, and the people discuss them, and testify to one another what the words have meant in their lives. But Rawsell would argue about every point, challenging this word or that, and he would always bring up the early writings— for instance the ones that said that blacks are descended from Cain. He was all for going back to the teachings of Joseph Smith and Parley Pratt and Brigham Young, and he didn't believe the doctrine that the modern Prophet, the head of the church, can receive new revelations that revise or supersede old teachings.

Finally the bishop talked to Rawsell and asked him not to speak in church if he couldn't be more positive about the modern situation. Rawsell, always headstrong and rigid, stalked out, and after that the Hetters didn't come to Sunday school at all. Reba told her mother that they had services at home and drew even closer. Even now, one saw, she still believed they had been right.

Next Rawsell took the children out of school, marched into their school one day and dragged them out. This was because the class was planning to study about Martin Luther King; to honor him thus conflicted with the early church idea that blacks descended from Cain, an idea that the contemporary Prophet had rescinded. Rawsell said he would teach his children himself. I didn't find these prejudices sympathetic for a martyr, but Volker excused Rawsell Hetter in view of the general drama of the man's obsessions and the tragedy of his end, and remarked that martyrs are often unsympathetic, difficult people in life.

We had seen the one-room schoolhouse he built at their place, on the left just as you come up the drive, painted red with a little bell tower on top. There Reba taught reading and history, Rawsell taught math and geography, and the kids helped their parents on the farm. At first this life seemed idyllic, but there were problems, above all financial. Rawsell lost some livestock, there was a bad crop year, and also, after he got in trouble at church, there were people who stopped bringing their things for him to repair. A lot of people in that community felt strongly about giving their custom to someone who didn't go along with the church teachings.

Reba was sick one winter, so sick that her mother went out there and taught the classes, though it went against her grain to do it. Rawsell wouldn't have the doctor. He prayed over Reba, he anointed her with oil he had consecrated as a member of the Melchizedek priesthood; but he would have no doctor. "The Lord will do as he sees fit," he would say. That's when many people's hearts hardened toward Rawsell. When others had turned against him, some had stood up for him for Reba's sake, and because he was a hard worker and a good father, and because Reba continued to be besotted with love for him. But he would not have the doctor. Reba was sick for months, and everyone was afraid it was cancer. She couldn't get out of bed. The oldest daughters, April and Margot, did the housework. Rowena was still too little, and anyway, Frank Murphy told us, Rowena was the fair-haired child, and never had taken her share of the hard work.

During Reba's illness, April, the oldest, was only eleven or so. She believed her mother was going to die. After school she'd help in the New Zion Diner in town, then she'd have to go home and get her little brothers and sisters ready for bed. Rawsell did the cooking, and Rickie, who ran the diner, used to send things home for them to eat that she had leftover, most often a pie. They were so poor that sometimes they didn't have enough to eat, but they had love and religious faith, whatever they called themselves. For by now they were excommunicated from the Mormon church.

The blow, of course, was that Rawsell came to believe in plural marriage, like the patriarchs of old. He had gone up in the woods and prayed, and then one day came in and told Reba that it was their duty to live the life of the primitive church and that meant that he should take another wife.

This was a terrible shock to Reba. She and Rawsell had been as close as a man and a woman could be, and now she was being made to suffer the torment of violent jealousy. She prayed constantly to God to let her be free from it, and eventually He did, just as He had done for all those good Mormon wives of olden days, reconciling them to their lots and even perhaps suggesting that the life of a plural wife had some advantages.

Her husband was marrying another woman, and there was no one she could talk to about her grief. She was cut off from the women's groups of the regular Mormon church, and the bishop, and if she'd gone to her mother, the mother would have just said, "I told you so." It was all anyone could do to keep from saying it, even Volker and I, after the fact.

It was only a month before Rawsell began building a little house alongside of the other, and announced he was going to marry Merrilyn Rice. Everyone knew her, the wife of Sandy Rice, a welder and sheet metal worker who lived in a trailer home outside of Marshall. Sandy Rice had walked out on her some years before.

"Is it true that, in polygamy, the husband has to take turns with each of his wives?" I had asked Frank Murphy.

"He has to treat them all equally, in principle," he said. I noticed that he used the present tense about polygamy, for of course it is a thing that still goes on, though I had thought only in renegade hill colonies or Arizona caves, not in plain little towns a few minutes from Salt Lake and Park City, and spoken of calmly by the respectable librarian.

"Did he treat them equally—Merrilyn and Reba?"

"She has always said so," Frank said. "It was about now that Reba had all her teeth pulled out. I think she really believes God is going to send her another set. It is in her nature to be fanatic, and to have burning beliefs."

The first night he stayed with Merrilyn, Reba said she felt more bitter and bleak than ever before in her life. She prayed, and she watched for the lights to go out over in Merrilyn's house, and at that moment wanted to die, and God did nothing to relieve her feelings. Volker and I were amazed by the cheerful and matter-of-fact way she spoke, now, of her husband's other wife, of her torment, and of how God intended this arrangement for men and women. People in Utah have a generally docile attitude to God, it seemed to us. I was fascinated by Reba; Volker was preoccupied by Rawsell's martyrdom, though to what cause he could not make me understand.

The next problem for the Hetters was with the school inspector, who found that the children were falling behind. The oldest two, April and Margot, were bright, but the younger boys and Rowena didn't pass the tests for their age groups. The state said: Either send them to school or we'll put them in a home. The situation seems not to have been handled very well by the authorities, who made themselves seem cruel and arbitrary; but the Hetters were also impossibly uncooperative. April told us that she planned, if they were taken, to run away, and she instructed her brothers and sisters in this. I imagined how it was for those children, thinking that strangers were going to take them away. And they were right, for that did happen, after the death of Rawsell.

The school inspector got a court order, and it was up to the sheriff to enforce it. The sheriff went to talk to Rawsell a number of times, but Rawsell continued to refuse, just said, Never, let them come and get me. How to do that was quite controversial in the community at the time. Some people said they ought to just go in and blast him out, other people thought the whole thing was overblown and advised just letting them alone, or sending them a visiting teacher.

At first, with the little children there, and the two women, the sheriff was reluctant to use force. He had the feeling Rawsell would resist, so he just said, Okay, take your time, I'm not coming on your land—but when you come out, I'll be waiting for you. And he posted his men to watch the place, figuring that somebody would have to go for food eventually. Then it got out of hand, to this day no one knows how, an example of the misguided aggression of men who couldn't endure defiance, in a state where people are generally compliant under the rule of an autocratic regime; or perhaps it was just the escalating logic of guns. The sheriff's deputies and some men from the Utah National Guard had a command post set up in a neighbor's garage. They even had men on snowmobiles guarding the pasture behind there, in case he tried to slip out over the snowfield. Afterward people said, "You'd have thought they had John Dillinger at bay in there."

Rawsell was carrying his gun, but it wasn't loaded. Some said he aimed it, some said he didn't. He had come down to get the mail, and he was carrying his gun. The deputies charged him and shot him. People heard later they shot him in the back, when he was walking back up to his house, as the family watched. Frank Murphy had photographs of the body with three holes in the back, but these pictures were never admitted into evidence at the inquiry.

With the press encamped outside during the siege, the whole denouement was captured on video—April, twelve years old, in pinafore and lace cap, running out of the house to shoot at her father's killers with her bow and arrows. I ran this sequence over and over, full of love for April's courage, and full of outrage over the grotesque militarism of the authorities.

The sheriff immediately jailed Reba, and took the children to Salt Lake to the juvenile facility. There they refused to eat, as April instructed them. Not even the littlest ones ate a morsel. I tried to imagine Reba having to look at Rawsell's body and then being put in jail herself—it seemed a gratuitously cruel sequence of events. There was an inquiry, which cleared the police, as these things always do; but the children never did go to school. Everyone felt ashamed after that, and the authorities dropped the whole issue, so in a way nothing had happened except that a man had died, and, if the children were badly off before, now it was worse, because Reba had no one, all those kids, and no money and no breadwinner. Volker and I differed about Reba; he thought she was saintly and heroic.

Back home, doing research for the script, I continued reading the history of the Mormon church, about the bloody persecutions and rowdy migrations, and mud and oxen and mobs. I had trouble with the idea of polygamy. Joseph Smith had introduced the practice in 1831, it became church doctrine in 1852, and it wasn't abolished until 1890, when it came down to a trade-off between statehood and wives. History seemed to show, to me at least, that Smith had invented polygamy to sanctify his roving eye, and his first wife, Emma, had been outspoken in her objections to it. His male followers took it up enthusiastically, though it brought an army down on them, and earned them a legacy of ridicule. Except for Emma, I found no names of women at all in the history, only men. I gazed at photos of hairy patriarchs with diverting names like Parley Parker Pratt and Lilburn W. Boggs. You could not but wonder how you would like to be a plural wife.

Our film about the Hetters proved impossible. Gracious and cooperative in person, Reba had proved less so when it came to having words put in her mouth in a script. Eventually Volker went back to Europe to work on something else. But after some months I again found myself in Park City, Utah, this time with J., for a meeting of his International Infectious Disease Council. We stayed in the Wasatch Inn, quintessence of Victorian charm, full of butter churns and candle molds and ferns and pancake breakfasts.

I had planned to phone Reba or April to propose a visit, but, on the evening of our arrival, we heard an item on the hotel television news: "Authorities are questioning Mrs. Patricia Hetter of Lopex in this morning's bombing of the

Mormon church in Marshall. Mrs. Hetter and members of her family have made several threats against the church in the past." The footage was of the house I knew, with knots of reporters standing around in the drive, then police walking out the front door with a tall woman between them, Reba, tossing her long hair. "Mrs. Hetter is the widow of Rawsell Hetter, who was killed ten years ago in a shoot-out with Utah state authorities. Hetter had defied court orders by refusing to let his children attend public schools. Her son-in-law Dallin Bond is also being questioned," said the TV voice. Now the camera focused on Dallin Bond, who followed Reba Hetter and the officers. He was saying something out of range of the TV recorder.

The group—Reba, Dallin, police—stood by the police car. Dallin Bond was the young, handsome man with a patriarchal, fanatic look to his hot brown eyes. I had met him before. Rowena, now slender again, came out of the house and stood next to her mother and Dallin. Something struck me as odd here, but I didn't know what. The camera drew closer. I expected that the accused would duck their heads, but instead Reba turned and smiled her macabre toothless smile right at the camera.

The TV image now changed to one of a bombed, burnt structure, its steeple intact, its windows broken. It was an ugly building, like a funeral parlor. The voice identified it as the damaged Mormon church in Marshall, Utah, which had sustained a blast, apparently from a bomb. This unattractive modern building seemed somehow an unworthy object of someone's vengeance, not equivalent to the life of a man.

The headline of the next morning's newspaper account said, HETTER WIDOW ADMITS GRUDGE BOMB. The piece explained that Reba had committed the bombing, on the tenth anniversary of the murder of her husband. Her statement claimed revenge for Rawsell's "murder by the Mormon Church." This I did not quite understand, since he had been killed by state troopers, but I could well see how a woman might hold a grudge, and indeed "grudge" seemed a ludicrous and trivial word for the feeling one would have against the killers of a beloved husband. We also learned that history was repeating itself in another way: now Reba Hetter and her family were refusing to give themselves up for the bombing of the church in Marshall and instead were barricaded, like ten years before, inside their house, awaiting the resurrection of Rawsell Hetter and the onset of the Final Days.

In the morning I could not resist driving my group of foreign visitors down the lane where the Hetter family had barricaded themselves in. It was a crisp autumn day. Sportive vehicles were parked on every side, giving the impression of a football Saturday. People were sitting in the cars or leaning in at the windows, talking. Police cars, a TV van marked KWEM, a Jeep Cherokee, a Ford pickup, a Sheriff Department four-wheel-drive Eagle parked crossways at the bottom of the Hetters' driveway by the mailbox to block any access in or out.

Various officials had made statements, chiefly to the effect that their patience was endless, they did not seek a repeat of the events of ten years ago, and that violence could not be condoned. The video showed the curtains drawn at the Hetter house, with little gaps where the besieged people would be peeking out to watch their would-be captors. I was absorbed in it. I pitied and almost admired the vengeful spirit of the woman inside, who had seen her husband shot in the back by these same burly men who surrounded her now, in checked wool jackets and hunting caps. But I thought too of a scene

I had once been watching on television when before our eyes the terrorists in a Los Angeles house were burned alive by police. That could happen here. With all these men and guns it was perhaps even likely to happen. The police response seemed overelaborate for a provocative but not very important act of arson. But, I also thought, she should not subject her children and the little grandchildren to the danger. A part of me that had not quite believed in her was now animated by doubt.

Inside the log house were the whole family—the mother, Reba Hetter; April Bond—the one who for some reason interested me most; her sister Rowena; the five or six little grandchildren; presumably the two younger Hetter boys, whose names nobody ever said; the son-in-law Dallin Bond; the paralyzed son, a circumstance that had not been explained; and perhaps other relatives. Outside, the locals in their wide Stetson hats and boots and holstered pistols were providing a good show, one familiar from western movies.

Watching it with me were three Japanese—Dr. Akira Kora, a short man with slightly bowed legs; Dr. Kora's wife; and Mrs. Kiko Kagura—the Thai Dr. Prangithornbupu, and Dr. Wurfel, a Swiss. Nothing about my foreign visitors gave much clue as to what they were thinking about the scene. Kiko Kagura looked fascinated but uncomfortable and apprehensive, while Dr. Prangithornbupu and Dr. Wurfel looked on with eager pleasure to think they were, or might be, within range of guns. So American. I was conscious, as I explained the history and implications of this local event, of taking the slightly proprietary tone of a tour guide. Like a conscientious leader, I herded my little group of IIDC visitors at a safe distance from the menacing police cars and heavy-thighed, leather-jacketed officers milling around in the driveway of the pretty, so prototypically American, log cabin, and I sounded to myself almost pleased that in America as in faraway places strange things can happen—desperate standoffs, exotic religions. There is a certain pleasure in the thought that strangeness is to be found in one's native land, a place you always think of as so plain. It reminded me that America is a rough, wild country, not so different today from a hundred years ago, with peculiar customs, suspicious tribes, sinister religions, and inhospitable regions in which a poorly prepared traveler can die. Richard Burton, the great explorer and expert on tribes, had been impelled by his explorer's need to cross an ocean and a continent to visit Utah, to observe the fascinating polygamous ancestors—not so distant—of April Bond; but what was exotic for Burton was still an issue for righteous Utahns. I had explained to my tourists, as I showed them the multidoored houses, that the neighbors of polygamists, while resenting them, usually tolerated and coped with them with resignation or charity, as if they were doing penance for the friskiness of their own bearded old rifle-toting, hypocrite forebears. Now they had trained guns on them.

"The people inside are criminals?" asked Mrs. Kora.

"Well, in a sense," I admitted, unable to think of a better definition. "They did commit a crime. They put a bomb in a church."

"Protest," said Dr. Kora knowledgeably. "This happens in Japan also." I nodded. I had once seen police beat protesters in Japan. The people had been protesting nuclear plants. What had charmed me was that the police helmets had the same form as the armor of the ancient samurai. It is interesting how images of authority remain imprinted on a society. I thought of Mountie hats and the Stetsons of these Utahns, and of the odd little pillboxes worn to this day by French gendarmes.

"What will happen?" Mrs. Kagura asked.

"The police will stay outside until the people have to come out. They'll try to talk them into coming out," I said. The travelers stared attentively at the front door, as if someone might emerge at any second, requiring some response from themselves.

"Real Mormons you say?" Dr. Kora asked again.

Though it was not possible to walk nearer the Hetter house, within range of gunfire, no effort was made to prevent us from milling around with the other sightseers and local people. Beyond the barricade, several men in uniforms could be seen conferring, their manner casual. Another, wearing a large hat, seemed to be photographing or surveying through a binocularlike instrument. We became aware of the approach of a helicopter overhead. Someone arrived in an Isuzu Trooper and pushed his way up to the barricade to speak to the police. Then he went around the barricade and walked up to the house.

"That's the father, Ralph Bond, Dallin's dad," someone said in the crowd.

Dr. Kora took many video feet of this picturesque American episode. I followed the direction of his viewfinder as it captured the log house, the heavy rifles of the police, their six-guns and cowboy hats. It was the hardware of American life that appeared to interest him, or the contrast of hardware and primitive emotions: nightscopes, telescopic sights, helicopters, loudspeakers, klieg lights. As my tour group went back to the car, I spoke to one of the television people, to ask if there was any new development in the situation.

"A psychologist is coming from Denver," he said.

I understood why Reba Hetter was barricading herself in, but I was also wondering why April Bond, a seemingly sensible young woman with young children to worry about, stayed in there. I wondered if she were a prisoner of the others. What must she feel about the danger to the little ones? I had liked April and could not get her out of my mind—her beauty and force, the hardness of her rural life, the battery of kids. About Reba Hetter, ostensible heroine of all this, something still troubled me, an unaccountable mistrust.

It was only then, as I stood there, that another bit of the puzzle slid into place, an unexpected detail did something to explain my feeling. It was a circumstance I should have but had not grasped the significance of before: April's husband was Dallin Bond, the handsome young man who had first loved her for her heroism when she was twelve. But, if I'd understood correctly, the handsome man in the plaid shirt standing by Reba and Rowena as they smiled at the cameras had been spoken of as the husband of Rowena. There were a number of possible explanations, but one was more peculiar and more shocking than the others, and the most plausible: that just as the martyred Rawsell had been the husband of two women, Dallin Bond was the husband of both April and Rowena, a fact that neither Reba, Frank Murphy the librarian, nor April herself had told us.

It seemed so crazy. Though I had mistrusted, I had almost liked Reba and now I almost hated her, for imposing her fanaticism on her daughters, and illiteracy unto the third generation, for the pretense of school had now been abandoned altogether, along with attempts by the community to rescue Rowena's and April's children. That was a worse crime than polygamy. To be fair, what was so terrible about polygamy anyhow, except that it denied to women what was allowed to men, erotic variety, the tacit recognition of erotic restiveness? An erotically restless person myself, I thought with sadness of those poor Mormon wives spending alternate cold nights, being visited like mares and left to cope with their children between times, with no help from the husband off in other pastures. Why were they so docile, those poor frontier women? I could sadden myself, thinking about it, feeling a lonely estrangement from the female sex of the nineteenth century, for being so limp and dauntless, and from the women of Utah today for the same reason. In the hotel, I told all this to J.: "The Dallin Bond they are talking about I think is the husband of both the daughters, father of all six children, and, as far as I can tell, sole support of the mother and brothers too."

"Poor bastard," said J.

Later I called Frank Murphy. "Yes, the husband of Rowena and April both," he said, "and some people are mean enough to say he's sealed to Reba too. I think that's going too far, but Reba does have a power over him. The men kid Dallin about his wives. They say, 'He took the bait, now he's on the hook.' "

"That's horrible," I cried. Now I could acknowledge that my irrational dislike for Reba Hetter was for allowing her daughters to feel the misery she herself must have felt. It was indignation on behalf of April Bond as I imagined how I would feel, sharing my husband, and thinking about the peculiar family life they must have, and how all this explained the forlorn quality of the place, April's air of neglect—explained her patience, perhaps, and her slightly flat response to events—her air, if it must be said, of passive compliance a little at odds with her seeming intelligence. I wondered if April felt the sort of rage that Reba had felt. "How could Reba let it happen to her daughters, after it happened to her?"

"They believe in it, don't forget," Frank said, and I could

see there was a discrepancy between me and him; I had thought that plural marriage was illegal and punishable, like moonshining or incest, but Utahns shrugged it off. "There are thousands like that, you know, down in southern Utah and Arizona. What are you going to do—put them all in jail?"

In my mind, as if for my script, I wrote scenes inside the house, and could not seem to take any point of view but April's. It wasn't that April hadn't believed her mama, who was always saying she expected Papa's resurrection, it was that she hadn't paid enough attention. And she hadn't realized how Dallin was always listening to Mama. April didn't know what Dallin believed, even though he said Amen when Mama prayed.

"It had to be done," Mama would say over and over. "God forgive us for not doing it sooner." She and Dallin would look at each other, exulting. She would say this to the television people and when people called on the phone, "It had to be done, God forgive us for not doing it sooner." People began to call right away. After the television people, the police came back, and April heard Dave Boyd, the police chief in Marshall, say, "We're going to prepare an indictment, Reba, and you'll have to come in, but we'll give you until tomorrow morning."

When the police and the camera people had left, Reba ate a sandwich, but, not sitting down, she strode around the kitchen, peering out the windows, and about dinnertime she said, "We'd better get some guns and ammunition, because I'm not going anywhere tomorrow, they'll have to come take us." They had two shotguns and two .22 rifles.

A little later, Mama called the police station. Rowena began to cry, which April could understand, despising it.

Rowena was remembering the other time, the weeks inside, the police outside, and she could foresee all the trouble, and the death at the end of it, like last time. Like last time. That was on all their minds. April didn't go outside to hear what Mama told the television people, but she could imagine it, and her thoughts were on what to do with the children. The babies shouldn't be here; April was prepared to defy Mama on that. After dinner, she sat in the window seat, thinking about it, and unfolded her patchwork. When the children tried to talk to her, she snapped at Rowena. "Can't you put them to bed? I had them all day." She had lost her thimble, and had to push her needle through with her forefinger, leaving little pricks, which didn't hurt but bled, and it seemed ominous. Each patch a remembered thing, mostly her own old clothes, then worn by Margot, then Rowena. It was Dallin's night to spend with Rowena, but he didn't move to go back to their house.

Reba and Dallin sat down in the kitchen and ate more sandwiches, and talked about demands, though, as far as April could see, it was not within the power of man to grant them. Man could not restore to the Hetter family what had been taken from it. What Mama really wanted was to call down trouble on the heads of their enemies, but it didn't seem to April that bombing the church would hurt them all that much. She had long ago accepted that she did not know the reason she was a member of this family and not some other, or why her family and not some other had been marked. She did not feel different from other people, she got along with others, in Lopex and Marshall both—with people at the store, with friends of Dallin from his high school. She'd lived here all her life. She did not even believe that Mama had some unique and unusual access to truth; it was that her family had adopted as true a set of beliefs that bound her, like the untouchables in India, or the gypsies. If you were a member of an outcast family, then you just were.

It was part of her love for Dallin that he had come into their outcast family and taken its problems on himself. He wouldn't have had to. His father had a good business in Marshall, he was a pillar of the Mormons. Brooding on the probable death of Dallin, April could not help but think about how she loved him, and how she had from the first minute, and how he said he had loved her first when he saw her on television, just a little girl, with a bow and arrows, going to defend her dad. I'm going to marry that girl, he had said. It was as fated a marriage as the marriage of Mama and Papa.

She thought about the first time they had made love. It had been beautiful. She had never asked Rowena or spoken of her nights with him. If Dallin had wanted another wife, April would have preferred some girl from Marshall, a stranger, even if she were prettier. She could not account for the pain it had given her that the wife was Rowena, the favorite of their mother, who always got what she wanted and never did what she didn't want to.

Mama put it in Rowena's head to want Dallin. Things had been beautiful before. They had their love, they had their babies, they had their boy that died, that Dallin had brought, a baby that had been too little, which was not Dallin's fault. If she had gone to the hospital, maybe that little one would not have died, but Dallin did the best he could, Mama too, but if only she had gone to the hospital. Rowena of course went to the hospital. Mama wouldn't let Dallin take any chances with Rowena, and why did Dallin want Rowena, she's just a silly girl, not as pretty either . . . Sometimes her thoughts, these same ones over and over, crowded so close to one another, like clothes in the washer, churning together, that she couldn't make them stop.

Later, she put the children to bed upstairs at Mama's house, and lay on a mattress in the attic room with the six little ones camped around her. They were fussy and sleepless. If Dallin died she would be alone forever. She could hear Mama and Dallin and Ted downstairs, Mama's voice raised, maybe in exhortation. She could imagine Mama down there tossing her beautiful hair, all gold still, like Rowena's. She thought of Mama braiding Rowena's golden hair and running her hands along it. She saw Mama tossing her hair, and pacing in the living room, and putting her hand on the back of Dallin's neck, then Ted's, a laying on of hands to firm them in their resolution. April could hear her little brother Ben pleading to have a gun, and Mama saying, "All right."

How smoothly they fell into the rhythm of the besieged. It was in all their minds that history would repeat itself, and that this meant that it would be Dallin who would be killed. Behind Reba's ritual cheerfulness lay, almost, this requirement. The police would storm, would kill Dallin, and his death would remind the world once again what they had suffered at the hands of their persecutors. Nonetheless they prayed aloud that this would not happen, and for courage.

In the bathroom, April prayed again that Dallin would not be killed, that she herself, even, or Rowena, or one of the boys but not Dallin or the children. She prayed for the ability to feel her mother's passion, which she had felt before, when Papa was killed, but did not feel now. She prayed that her father would rise as Mama predicted, if only for a minute, so that Mama would be proved right and all this would be over.

. . .

The suspense in any case was not long. Coming back from a mountain hike the next morning, we saw that the morning papers had arrived on the front desk at the Wasatch Inn. The headlines said, TRAGIC END TO HETTER STANDOFF. I dropped into a chair in the lobby to read, hardly able to bear the moment until I learned whether someone had been killed, and who. But I was surprised to read that it was a National Guard deputy, Andy Frame, age thirty-four, wounded in the neck by gunfire when deputies had attempted to storm the house Friday night. He had died that morning in the Park City General Hospital, killed by a .22 bullet fired by someone in the Hetter house. The bullet had unfortunately severed his jugular vein. With that, the Hetters had surrendered, shaken and fearful that the sheriff would now bomb them or burn them out. There were photographs of Andy Frame, taken in high school or college, a thin-necked, smiling boy with a hairline already high. Another photograph showed Dallin Bond and a second male being put in a police car. The article explained that the whole family had been arrested.

Our week at an end, I was obliged to follow the Hetter trial in the San Francisco newspapers, which with their usual infidelity left great gaps in my knowledge until the sentencing, which was mentioned in a tiny item in the back. Reba Hetter and Dallin Bond had been convicted of second-degree murder, and one of the sons, Ted Hetter, of conspiracy. This seemed both sad and fitting—sad especially for April and Rowena, and their now fatherless six children. How would they live? What could they do? Feeling still strangely involved, I sent a small check to April, from a "well-wisher." I didn't want to send anything to Rowena, who had accepted her sister's husband, though I should have felt more charitable toward that poor child. To me, Reba

Hetter seemed beyond wickedness, leading her children down this path, and killing the person named Andy.

The Salt Lake papers gave a fuller account of the case, but failed to mention a detail that surprised me but should not have. Frank Murphy told me April had accused Dallin. Though there was a law that wives need not testify against their husbands, she said she was bound to the truth. She said that it had been Dallin who killed the deputy. Then Rowena had contradicted her sister, saying it had been her brother Ted. "It was Ted that did it," Rowena said again and again. "April wasn't even in the room, she was upstairs with me and the babies. Why would she say it was Dallin?"

No one believed her, a simple sixteen-year-old in love with Dallin. It was April's sacrifice of him for the sake of truth that impressed them.

I reserved to myself my guess about the truth of the matter. The people in Utah didn't seem to want to speak of certain emotions: how you would feel when your husband lay in the arms of your sister. I wondered if it were only I who was jealous and proprietary, reading into something elemental about religion and truth something citified and petty about sexual jealousy; for it seemed to me that Reba Hetter had encouraged Rawsell Hetter to his death because he had betrayed her, and then April had put her false husband in prison, and that this was all a tale of female revenge. And what to me had seemed to be about revenge had seemed to the Hetters themselves a religious drama fraught with implications for eternity. What the role of the Mormon church was in all this I could not say, but probably female revenge accounts in the world for more misfortune than people think. The realization gave me a forlorn sense of satisfaction.

Of course I knew that Reba Hetter would think I hadn't

got it at all. She would say my understanding was limited, a godless city dweller's banal perception, feet in the mud of Freud, pop psych, away from God, without principles or passions, devoid of metaphysics or a sense of damnation. I hadn't got it at all, she would think. But does a traveler ever really get it, traveling through, wondering and wishing to be home as dramas and deaths unfold, and then, at home, getting the impulse to voyage out again, even if just to Utah, a place as strange as Afghanistan? As Calvino might have said, you bring to a new place only the little you know, and take home not much more than a sense of the strangeness of everything, but of the sameness too, so that, as curious as things are, you are never quite a stranger.

A NOTE ON THE TYPE

The text of this book is set in Garamond No. 3.
It is not a true copy of any of the designs of Claude Garamond (1480–1561), but an adaptation of his types, which
set the European standard for two centuries. It probably
owes as much to the designs of Jean Jannon, a Protestant
printer working in Sedan in the early seventeenth century,
who had worked with Garamond's romans earlier, in Paris,
and who was denied their use because of the Catholic censorship. Jannon's matrices came into the possession of the
Imprimerie Nationale, where they were thought to be by
Garamond himself, and so described when the Imprimerie
revived the type in 1900. This particular version is based on
an adaptation by Morris Fuller Benton.

Composed by PennSet, Inc.,
Bloomsburg, Pennsylvania
Printed and bound by Haddon
Craftsmen, Scranton, Pennsylvania
Designed by Mia Vander Els